★ TELEPATHY
★ CLAIRVOYANCE
★ PRECOGNITION

Have you ever known the identity of a telephone caller—even before the phone rang? Or had thoughts about someone and later found out they were thinking about you at that *exact moment?*

Nearly all of us have had such experiences—but how many times have we mistakenly chalked them off as a matter of chance. But are they really?

Now you can find out for sure simply by using the technique outlined in this book, most of them carefully researched and developed at the world-famous Institute for Parapsychology in Durham, N. C.

Learn how to recognize a genuine ESP experience . . . discover what turns it on . . . and how it may be heightened.

YOU MAY HAVE MENTAL POWERS YOU KNOW NOTHING ABOUT

⊘ SIGNET (0451)

MIND POWER

- ☐ **THE POWER OF ALPHA THINKING: Miracle of the Mind by Jess Stearn.** Through his own experiences and the documented accounts of others, Jess Stearn describes the technique used to control alpha brain waves. Introduction by Dr. John Balos, Medical Director, Mental Health Unit, Glendale Adventist Hospital. (141911—$3.95)

- ☐ **SELF-MASTERY THROUGH SELF-HYPNOSIS by Dr. Roger Bernhardt and David Martin.** A practicing psychoanalyst and hypnotherapist clears up many misconceptions about hypnosis (it is not a form of sleep, but actually is a state of heightened awareness), and shows how to put it to use as a therapeutic tool in everyday life. (141008—$2.95)

- ☐ **SELF HYPNOTISM: The Technique and Its Use in Daily Living by Leslie M. LeCron.** Using simple, scientifically proven methods, this guidebook provides step-by-step solutions to such problems as fears and phobias, overcoming bad habits, pain and common ailments, and difficulty with dieting—all through the use of self-suggestion therapy.
(137396—$3.50)

- ☐ **TRANSCENDENTAL MEDITATION by Maharishi Mahesh Yogi.** The new prophet of worldwide peace, who believes that "the natural state of man is joy," describes his simple technique of deep meditation.
(140818—$4.95)

- ☐ **DAVID ST. CLAIR'S LESSONS IN INSTANT ESP by David St. Clair.** Through astoundingly simple techniques, discovered and perfected by a recognized authority on ESP, you can learn how incredibly gifted you are—and put your gifts to practical and permanent use to enrich and expand your life.
(140494—$2.95)

*Prices slightly higher in Canada

Buy them at your local bookstore or use this convenient coupon for ordering.

NEW AMERICAN LIBRARY,
P.O. Box 999, Bergenfield, New Jersey 07621

Please send me the books I have checked above. I am enclosing $_____ (please add $1.00 to this order to cover postage and handling). Send check or money order—no cash or C.O.D.'s. Prices and numbers are subject to change without notice.

Name_____

Address_____

City_____ State_____ Zip Code_____

Allow 4-6 weeks for delivery.
This offer is subject to withdrawal without notice.

Test Your ESP

Edited by MARTIN EBON

Contributors:
Robert Brier
Henie Brier
Eleanore Gohdes
Joyce Jones

A SIGNET BOOK
NEW AMERICAN LIBRARY

Copyright © 1970 by Martin Ebon

All rights reserved.

SIGNET TRADEMARK REG. U.S. PAT. OFF. AND FOREIGN COUNTRIES
REGISTERED TRADEMARK—MARCA REGISTRADA
HECHO EN CHICAGO, U.S.A.

SIGNET, SIGNET CLASSIC, MENTOR, ONYX, PLUME, MERIDIAN AND NAL BOOKS *are published by New American Library, Inc., 1633 Broadway, New York, New York 10019*

FIRST PRINTING, JANUARY, 1971

9 10 11 12 13 14 15 16

Printed in U.S.A.

FOREWORD

DEAR READER:

As a writer and speaker on the subject of extrasensory perception, or ESP, I am constantly being asked, "Where can I have my ESP tested?" Those who put this question usually assume that their potential gifts of clairvoyance, telepathy or precognition (foreknowledge) should be put to the test through a series of complex experiments, against a background of flashing lights, humming computers and forbidding-looking statistical charts. While these paraphernalia are, indeed, part of the laboratory setting for a good deal of ESP testing, they are not essential to the kind of experiment that the average person might want to undertake.

It isn't the equipment that counts. What matters are the controls exercised during a test, and just how the results are evaluated. You can arrange perfectly tight and scientifically acceptable experiments in your own living room. Just make sure you follow the techniques outlined in this book. If you do, your results can be more solid than those achieved with a battery of computers but lacking in experimental care.

The experimental methods used in this volume are mainly those developed by the Institute for Parapsychology of Durham, North Carolina. The Institute is part of the Foundation for Research on the Nature of Man, successor of the well-known Parapsychology Laboratory which functioned from 1927 to 1965 at Duke University. Dr. J. B. Rhine, who directed the Duke Laboratory and now heads the F.R.N.M., stated in the symposium *Parapsychology: From Duke to FRNM* (Durham, 1965) that "public interest in parapsychology seems to be a steady development in itself, rather than a passing flurry or fad." However until now, laboratory work has been so demanding that staff members of the Institute for Parapsychology simply have not found time to communicate their experiences and methods to the general public. This book should act as a bridge across this gap.

I am listing, below, the names and affiliations of those who contributed to this volume. Knowing the work load every one of them had to carry, I am doubly grateful for their diligent and enthusiastic collaboration. Although this book is not a publication of the Institute, readers may wish to address queries concerning additional experimental work to the *Institute for Parapsychology, Box 6847, Durham, N. C. 27708;* additional details can be found in the concluding chapter of this volume.

MARTIN EBON

New York, N.Y.
September, 1969

Contributors to this Volume

ROBERT BRIER has been a Research Fellow at the Foundation for Research on the Nature of Man, Institute for Parapsychology, from 1965 to the present. He is co-editor, with Dr. J. B. Rhine, of *Parapsychology Today* (New York, 1968) and has contributed a number of papers to the *Journal of Parapsychology*. A lecturer and researcher, he is a member of the Parapsychological Association. As this book goes to press, Bob Brier is completing his Ph.D. in Philosophy at the University of North Carolina, Chapel Hill. He acted as editorial coordinator for this volume and contributed the chapters entitled "How to Investigate a 'Haunted House,'" "Yes, There Is Negative ESP," and "What Next?".

HENIE BRIER, who wrote the majority of chapters in *Test Your ESP*, is a former staff member of the Institute for Parapsychology. She has lectured on parapsychology and has written technical as well as popular articles on the subject. She is the wife of Bob Brier; they have two children. Henie Brier contributed the chapters entitled "Everyone Has ESP," "Are You a 'Sheep' or a 'Goat'?," "The ABC's of ESP Testing," "Testing for Children," "Mind over Matter," and "Party Games with ESP."

viii   TEST YOUR ESP

ELEANORE GOHDES, a graduate of Duke University and former staff member of the Institute for Parapsychology, contributed the chapter entitled "Test Your Pet."

JOYCE JONES, a graduate of Atlantic Christian College, Wilson, N. C., and a former staff member of the Institute for Parapsychology, wrote the chapter on "Testing with Photographs."

Contents

	Foreword: Dear Reader	v
	Contributors to This Volume	vii
Chapter I:	Everyone Has ESP	11
Chapter II:	Are You a "Sheep" or a "Goat"?	23
Chapter III:	The ABC's of ESP Testing	31
Chapter IV:	Tests for Children	46
Chapter V:	Testing with Photographs	55
Chapter VI:	Test Your Pet	60
Chapter VII:	Yes, There is "Negative" ESP	75
Chapter VIII:	Party Games with ESP	83
Chapter IX:	Mind over Matter	92
Chapter X:	How to Investigate a "Haunted House"	99
Chapter XI:	What Next?	111
	Afterword: Can You Communicate Drawings? *by Andrea Fodor Litkei*	117
	Suggested Readings	137
	Glossary	139
	An ESP Record Sheet	143

CHAPTER I

Everyone has ESP

You have possibly marveled at some self-styled "psychic"—appearing before a television camera or on a platform—and wondered, "Could I do that?" If you turn to the science of parapsychology for an answer, you will find out that extrasensory perception is not the exclusive property of a few specially gifted persons. No one has a monopoly on ESP. It is an ability common to all of us, not the special hunting ground of famous clairvoyants, or of any other select group, such as indentical twins or exotic swamis.

You can also forget about claims that link the scientific study of ESP with magical hocus-pocus, or with an old-fashioned supernatural world of "ghosts" or "spirits." We have come a long way down the road from superstition to laboratory methods. In this jet age, yesterday's mystical beliefs have been reevaluated by hardheaded researchers. Many of the supposedly "supernatural" phenomena of past ages are now regarded as examples of everyday ESP—a strictly nonmagical capacity which we all share.

ESP is so common, in fact, that year after year thousands of ordinary people take the time to record their experiences and report them to parapsychology laboratories. These cases—called spontaneous experiences—come from housewives, salesmen, doctors, lawyers and possibly even Indian chiefs. Perhaps not all the reports are accurate, but we can safely assume that neither are all these people having hallucinations or making up stories. Such experiences, recorded throughout the history of man, initiated the scientific investigation of ESP phenomena in England about a hundred years ago.

How does one recognize a spontaneous ESP experience? What should one look for? There is one basic and important question which must be answered: Did the experience yield new and accurate information which could not have been known by means of the senses and which could not have been anticipated ordinarily?

Dr. Louisa E. Rhine, wife of Dr. J. B. Rhine, has studied many spontaneous experiences at the Institute for Parapsychology in Durham, North Carolina. She has one of the most extensive collections of these cases—over 12,000 of them—sent in by interested laymen. Here is one as reported in her book, *ESP in Life and Lab* (New York, 1967). Look for the new information:

"Several years ago, I lived in Virginia. One evening after dark, my wife fell down a long flight of stairs, breaking her left arm above the wrist. The next morning my daughter, living in Colorado, complained to her husband that her left arm pained her awfully and that she could see nothing but Mother. I wrote them about the accident. My daughter came immediately to Virginia to care for her mother. She stayed just a month. I took her to the train, which left at 10:45 a.m. She was now on the way back to Colorado. That evening while doing the chores around sundown, a wasp stung me in the right eyelid.

"The next morning my eye was swollen entirely shut and was very painful. As soon as my daughter arrived home, she reported as follows: "Dear Mamma, I had a nice trip home and found the folks all well. But what is the matter with Daddy's eye? My right eye is paining me so I can hardly stand it, and I can see nothing but Daddy. I don't think he is blinded, but his eye is swollen shut. Write me at once."

In this case, it seems that the daughter did gain the knowledge of her parents' afflictions through ESP. The daughter could not have known of her parents' troubles through ordinary sensory means, because she had not been in contact with her family.

Perhaps the most common kind of sympathetic pain is the sympathetic labor pain. Those close to the expectant mother may actually feel painful contractions when she is in labor—even if they do not know that she is in labor, or that she is expecting a baby. It is not safe to assume that sympathetic labor pains are impossible. ESP makes possible many "impossibilities"; as, for example, in this case, published by Dr. Louisa E. Rhine in an article, "Subjective Forms of Spontaneous Psi Experiences" (*Journal of Parapsychology,* June, 1953):

"Here is a very recent experience of my daughter, the wife of an army officer. Last Autumn they returned from a two-year duty tour in Germany. They left behind their older daughter who had married a young officer whose term overseas had not yet ended. Our granddaughter announced the arrival on January 9th at 11:30, in Germany, of the most beautiful baby boy in the world.

"To avoid useless anxiety, she had not told us on this side of her prospects, but on January 9th, her mother in Baltimore experienced the pains of childbirth, backache and bearing down, so severe and similar that the thought occurred to her that her daughter might be experiencing the actuality and she made a record of the time. When the report came as above, the time was found to be the same."

Parents and their children often seem to have an extrasensory rapport. In her first book, *Hidden Channels of the Mind* (New York, 1961), Mrs. Rhine indicates that preschool-age children are more likely to exhibit ESP than are older children. Younger children, whose limited lives center so completely around their parents, are often adept at expressing out loud the word, name, question or thought which a parent has been thinking. This thought communication is known as telepathy.

In a letter to the Institute for Parapsychology,

a woman reports what happened when she deliberately tried to impose a thought upon her daughter.

"When my daughter was small, she seemed to answer what I was thinking about. To prove it to myself, I deliberately thought of a friend of ours who lived far away and whom she had not seen very often. He had a habit of pinching the tip of his tongue between his lips when writing or studying; this was my thought. She looked up at me and said, 'Mommy, Ted always does this, doesn't he?' She pinched her tongue exactly as he did. I had this kind of thing happen quite often."

Here the woman seems to have successfully communicated with her child, telepathically, without speaking or using any ordinary means of communication. However, she had to be very careful that she didn't inadvertently or subconsciously pinch her own tongue between her lips while she was concentrating on this characteristic. This would have been a sensory (visual) cue.

While some individuals may excel at telepathy (the ability to know someone else's thoughts), others may excel at helping friends and family by using another ESP skill, clairvoyance. Clairvoyance is a term which describes knowledge by ESP of objects or events. Here is a typical case of clairvoyance, quoted by Mrs. Rhine in *Hidden Channels of the Mind*. The woman involved had placed her rings on a shelf near her kitchen sink; this is her experience:

"It was a warm day and remained warm into

evening," the woman relates, "so we decided to have a wiener roast outside. I got busy with preparations for that and forgot all about my rings. Later, after the children were in bed, I thought about my rings and went to get them. They were gone. I felt faint. My husband helped me look. We looked through all the garbage. I took everything off the shelf where I had put them. We even looked under the dining room and living room rugs. I swept every inch of the kitchen and no rings. It was getting late by this time and my husband was tired, so he went to bed. He wanted me to stop looking and get some rest, but I told him I couldn't sleep until I found my rings.

"This doesn't seem possible, but it happened! I was standing at the kitchen sink, trying to hold back my tears, and suddenly something told me to look in the ice cube tray. I rushed to the refrigerator, pulled out the ice cube tray and there were my rings, frozen in a cube of ice. I was so happy I rushed back to tell my husband. We started talking it over and he remembered coming into the house in the dark and without turning on the lights he opened the refrigerator, pulled out the ice tray for ice and reached for some glasses into the cupboard where my rings were. Then he filled the ice tray with water again and put it back in the refrigerator. He had never replaced a tray of ice before or since. Just that one time he replaced the ice tray. He didn't know my rings were on that shelf. I remember at the time I received the message, or whatever it was, I had a funny sensation. What made me look in that ice tray?"

In this case, the woman located her rings by using her ESP. But, we cannot categorize this case as telepathy because it is unlikely that she gained the knowledge through mind-to-mind communication. Her husband did not realize that in the dark room he had misplaced the rings. This, therefore, can be categorized as a case of clairvoyance, or ESP of an object (in this case, the unusual location of the rings). The objects in clairvoyance, of course, vary greatly and can be of any kind.

A study of spontaneous experiences shows that ESP does not follow ordinary rules of the conceivable or acceptable. It goes beyond the ordinary and easily believed to the unconventional and exciting. But ESP appears to be a perfectly normal capacity which everyone has.

Some people exhibit their ability often; they have numerous spontaneous experiences or they may consistently score high on ESP tests. Others exhibit ESP only under special conditions. Favorable conditions are more or less the same for each individual. A pleasant, quiet and relaxed atmosphere seems to work best.

Many women report having had spontaneous experiences (intuitions or hallucinations) while, say, washing dishes. This mechanical and routine kind of task encourages the rambling daydreaming during which ESP often manifests itself. Most men probably have their moments of daydreaming and gifted intuitions, too. But in our society it is the woman's prerogative to exercise her "woman's intuition." Men may feel more inhibited about discussing or reporting their experiences, or they may be more likely to brush them off as unusual coincidences. Thus we hear more cases from women than from men.

ESP results challenge today's physicists to broaden their concepts of space and time. Neither distance nor space seems to inhibit or affect ESP ability. The following case, also from Dr. Rhine's files, illustrates the fact that ESP does not appear to be limited by great distances (the writer was in America):

"My very young daughter was working with the United Nations in Korea before the Korean War. At that time people hardly knew where Korea was on the map. She was the only woman traveling around on trains with a group of men, setting up election booths, getting ready for the free election. The details of their time there are long since forgotten. But she was there and very far away.

"One morning I woke up with a slight feeling, 'Alice might call me today,' although I knew that this was a very long telephone call. This feeling persisted through the day and I did a lot of things and ran around being made very restless by it. Late in the afternoon, I stopped in at the house of her grandmother who was ill and blue and begged me to stay to dinner with her and help her pass the evening. 'No, Mother, I can't. I have the idea that Alice will call me tonight.' And Mother, although she was stiff about most things, said, 'If you feel so, then she will call!' I went home.

"Well, when I got inside my front door, the knowledge of her call hit me like a thunderbolt.

It was not guesswork, or hoping, or wishful thinking; it was pure, direct knowledge. I was unable to eat and for some reason was exhausted. I went to bed and finally thinking I might go to sleep, I left the light on near me. I fell heavily asleep. At 11 p.m. the telephone rang (I knew, of course, what it was) and it took twenty minutes for the various controls to connect up with one another and then came the little voice so clear, 'Hello, Mother—are you surprised?'

"The point about the sure knowledge is the greater because Alice herself did not know that she was going to call me that evening. It turned out that someone else who was going to call America couldn't do so for some reason and Alice at the last minute substituted her call. In short, I knew long before she did that she would call."

Case after spontaneous case, as well as laboratory experiments, have proven that ESP operates over vast distances with apparently no diminution of effect. It can cross distance; what about time? Man has shown the ability to know the future accurately. This ability is called precognition. Thus the three basic ESP capacities can be separated as follows: (a) telepathy, (b) clairvoyance, (c) precognition.

Precognition is often manifested in a dream that comes true. Every day and every night people dream or daydream of specific future events. The details are often startling, as in this tragic experience taken from the case files of the Institute for Parapsychology:

"Years ago, I dreamed one night that our 18-year-old son, with three other boys from the church which I was pastoring, had a car wreck at an intersection in which he was thrown out on the wet pavement and critically injured. The dream was so real that I woke myself up crying. I jumped out of bed and ran upstairs and switched on the light in his room and he was sound asleep, with his blond wavy hair out on the pillow and was the loveliest sight I have ever seen. I fell down on my knees by the bed and grabbed him and half drug him out of bed. He awoke good naturedly as he always did and said, 'Dad, did you have a nightmare?' I said, 'No, Ralph, it was worse than that for it seemed so real. I just dreamed that you were killed in a car wreck, and I just want you to know that I don't think I could go on without you.'

"I lay down on the bed by him for an hour and told him how I appreciated him and the fact that he had never seemed to shrink from any embarrassment at being a preacher's boy. He was planning on going to college that fall. I told him many things about how I appreciated him, the fact that he had never given us any trouble, and things I had locked up in my heart for years.

"About a month later, he, with the same three that I had seen in my dream, were in a car wreck as I had seen it. He was broken to pieces and lived five days. He was conscious and talked to us and then his noble spirit slipped across the line of worlds. I don't know if it was a warning that it could have been avoided had I asked him to discontinue keeping company with these boys. Only God knows. Maybe I will never know until I get to the judgment. But one thing I know—it did afford me the opportunity to say a lot of things to him that I wouldn't have otherwise, and I am grateful for that."

Precognitive experiences are not always sad. One case—another previously unpublished case from the Institute's file—has an amusing and ironic twist:

"A teenage girl was walking to her father's tailoring shop one afternoon and she passed by a large and unusual car, which she recognized to be a converted hearse. The large black automobile was parked across the street from the town drug store. Although there was no one near the car at the time, her intuition led her to believe that two men had driven the car into town and that these men intended to rob the drug store.

"When she arrived at her father's shop, she told her father and some other men who were present of her feelings. They, of course, laughed at her prediction. But she insisted that she was right and added that there would be a thunderstorm in a half hour (at the time it was clear and sunny) and at that time the drug store would be robbed. Sure enough, about a half hour later in the midst of a sudden thunder shower, the drug store was robbed. What's more, one of the men who had overheard the girl's story had gone to the druggist to have another laugh over the silly premonition. He was also robbed and he lost $300."

In a sense, we are all potentially amateur fortune tellers. Some people capitalize on their ability, making it seem as though their psychic powers are almost unlimited and infallible. But this is never the case. ESP in spontaneous experiences, as well as in test situations, is as whimsical, delicate and capricious as a spoiled child; but it responds well to patience, confidence and enthusiasm.

What is to be gained from your efforts in coaxing and patronizing this spirited capacity? To say the least, a good deal of excitement for everyone.

CHAPTER II

Are You a "Sheep" or a "Goat"?

Perhaps the most exciting moments in the history of ESP research came with the establishment of the Parapsychology Laboratory of Duke University. This laboratory, under the direction of Dr. J. B. Rhine, began to follow up spontaneous experiences and mediumistic phenomena with carefully controlled experiments. It operates today as an independent foundation, the Foundation for Research on the Nature of Man (F.R.N.M.); the Institute for Parapsychology is one branch of the Foundation.

The procedures that Dr. Rhine's laboratory pioneered are still the most basic and widely established means of testing for ESP. One group of tests makes use of a special deck of 25 ESP cards. This deck is made up of pictures of geometric shapes which are easy to remember.

Figure 1

There are 5 circles, 5 crosses, 5 wavy lines, 5 squares and 5 stars (see Figure 1). Testing with these cards involves using ESP to *know* the order of the 25 shuffled face-down cards. By sheer guesswork—over a number of trials—one should identify 5 cards out of 25. Each correct identification is called a "hit."

Are You a "Sheep" or a "Goat"? 25

The original work at the Parapsychology Laboratory resulted in many exciting discoveries. One of these involved a man named Hubert Pearce. Pearce was a young Methodist divinity student in Duke University's School of Religion, back in the early 1930's. His consistent high scoring made him one of the best ESP subjects ever tested. Pearce was chosen to be tested because spontaneous experiences were commonplace, not to him, but to his mother and other members of his immediate family.

Everything was new and fascinating in those days. The enthusiasm and excitement which accompanied the birth and growth of this new science must have been a tremendous inspiration to Pearce. His scores, though mediocre at first, soon skyrocketed and then stayed up there. He averaged scores 5 or 10 hits higher than could be expected through chance. The odds against these consistently high scores are billions to one. In other words, only once in several billion series of ESP tests would one expect such high results by chance alone. Since it is not likely that this was the one case in several billion, the scientific case for ESP seemed to be established.

Although Pearce was always tested with ESP cards, a little girl named Amy, another excellent ESP subject, worked almost exclusively with regular decks of 52 playing cards.

Dr. John Freeman, the parapsychologist who investigated Amy's case, reports that Amy and her family became aware of her ESP ability when Amy, then 9 years old, was confined to the house because of a bad cold. In his article about Amy in the *Journal of Parapsychology*, Dr. Freeman writes, "To keep her entertained, she had been given a deck of cards, and she discovered that she could tell what they were without looking at them. She had shown this to her mother, saying she had learned a 'new trick.' Later that evening she had repeated her performance for her father. Thinking she might have marked the cards in some way, he purchased a new deck. But the child was able to identify those, too, even when he himself held the cards, and even after he went into an adjoining room to shuffle and hold them."

When Dr. Freeman went to visit the family to test Amy, she correctly identified 24 cards out of the regular deck of 52, by both number and suit. Have you ever tried to identify a card, or 52 cards, simply by guessing? Can you imagine the odds against guessing the exact number and suit of 24 cards, the correct number for 9 others, and the correct suit for another 9 cards? The chances against this feat are millions to one. Amy only completely missed on 10 cards out of 52.

Can we be sure there was no trick involved? I think so. First of all, Amy never handled the cards. Therefore, there was no way that she could have shuffled or arranged them or memorized their order. Second, only after she named the top card, the target card, was it turned over and removed from the deck. So, it is not possible that she ever caught even a quick glimpse of the card before she made her guess. All standard playing cards are opaque; that is, it is impossible to identify the cards simply by looking at the backs, because they are not transparent.

Amy's high scoring did not go on forever. The last time she was tested by Dr. Freeman, when she was 12 years old, her scores were not at all exceptional. In fact, they corresponded exactly to chance guessing. But we cannot assume that her previous performances were just freak coincidences. The odds against her original spectacular rate of success are (as with Pearce) astronomical. Rather than assume that her performance is the one in millions that would appear by chance, it is more reasonable to assume that Amy's high scores were due to ESP.

The loss of ESP ability is common even in the best ESP subjects. Only if interest and motivation are sustained at a high pitch is a subject likely to continue to be a high scorer. The successful ESP subject works against tremendous pressure. With each new test of his ability, he is more or less staking the whole of his reputation. A great actor can almost always give at least a good performance because he consciously controls his body and voice. In a single performance, the great ESP subject must rely solely on his ability to intuit accurately. No matter how good the subject or how reliable his ability may seem, he has no conscious control over the operation of his ability. A low score in the midst of high scores is just as baffling to the subject as it is to the observer. He has no way of knowing why his ability veered off course, or how he can reorient himself to score high once again.

It is interesting to note that after Amy's scores

had dropped, she made a perfect score while visiting her grandmother. At that time, Amy was anxious to show her grandmother how well she could call cards, and once again she successfully identified the entire deck. Perhaps she succeeded on this day, while she had failed on others, because her motivation was stronger than usual. She sought to please her grandmother and to be the center of attention once again. Also, unlike the occasions when she was working with Dr. Freeman, who was relatively a stranger to her, at her grandmother's house she was surrounded only by her family.

Children, as a rule, score better than adults on ESP tests because they are not limited by notions that ESP is an unusual or even a nonexistent ability. A small child accepts the reality of ESP and his attempts to make accurate guesses are totally without inhibition. On the other hand, adolescents and adults are apt to be very self-conscious while they are guessing. This is understandable. They feel silly trying to succeed at a task which they have been made to believe is impossible. Thus, the child who is inspired by the challenge of the ESP test or game and perhaps by some small reward, has greater confidence in his ability to do well, and is more likely to make good, extrachance, scores.

Challenges and rewards are often related to high scoring. Pearce made his only perfect score when Dr. J. B. Rhine challenged him to do so by a playful $100.00 bet made on each card.

At New York City's Hunter College a psychology professor, B. F. Reiss, was challenged by his

Are You a "Sheep" or a "Goat"? 29

class to investigate ESP. He agreed to do so when the class claimed to have found a girl (she remains anonymous) whose abilities seemed promising. Here is how he set up his experiment:

1. The subject (the girl being tested) was situated in a room in one of the college buildings.

2. The experimenter and the target cards were located in a building 500 yards away.

3. Their watches were synchronized.

4. The experimenter looked at each of the 25 ESP cards at a specified time. At the same time, the subject concentrated on that target and recorded her guess.

Seventy-two runs (a run equals 25 card guesses) were completed after many sessions. An average score of 5 hits would be expected through chance. This subject averaged 18 hits per run. This is one of the most startling exhibits of ESP in the history of experimental testing. There was one perfect score of 25 hits in this series of 72 runs. Unfortunately, the tests had to be discontinued when the subject became ill.

In the language of parapsychology, those who believe in ESP are affectionately called "sheep." Those who do not believe in ESP, or those who are skeptical, are referred to, less affectionately, as "goats." Oddly enough, a person's attitude toward ESP seems to determine how well he will perform on ESP tests. Sheep are usually high scorers, while goats usually score below chance. Low—subchance—scores are also indicative of ESP. It is just as difficult to maintain scores 3 or 4 points below chance as it is to maintain scores 3 or 4 points above chance. On a series of standard ESP tests, again, the chances are that a person will average 5 hits. A low-scoring subject may never have more than 5 hits and may usually score 3, 2, 1 or no hits in a run. This subject, perhaps a very strong goat (or possibly a very strong sheep who has become too emotionally involved in his efforts to score well), is unconsciously using his ESP ability to select the wrong guess.

Although parapsychologists are no longer specifically seeking exceptional subjects like Amy and Hubert Pearce, it is always fun to discover someone who seems to be a natural. If you know any "sheep" who has a great confidence in his ability and is happy and excited at the prospect of being tested, you may be dealing with a truly gifted individual. Could you be one? See the next chapters for simple experiments by which you can test yourself, your friends and your family.

CHAPTER III

The ABC's of ESP Testing

To conduct your own ESP tests, follow these three steps:

A. Get on your mark—by deciding what type of ESP you want to test.

B. Get set—by preparing the materials you'll need.

C. Go—actual testing, step by step.

Get on your mark—Try the following Clairvoyance Tests:

It is simple to test for clairvoyance. There are two or three basic card tests. In one method, called the "Basic Technique," or "BT" for short, the cards are isolated one by one when the person makes his guesses. In the second method, the cards are stacked up and the subject guesses "Down Through" the deck (DT). This second method is better because it eliminates the possibility of catching a glimpse of

Name: John Smith Date 10/28 No. 1
Type of test: Clairvoyance (DT)

Call	Card	Call	Card	Call	Card	Call	Card	Call	Card
1 H	S	C	C						
2 S	C	H	H						
3 C	C	S	D						
4 D	H	D	D						
5 D	D	C	S						
6 C	S	C	C						
7 H	D	C	C						
8 D	S	H	D						
9 H	C	S	H						
10 C	H	S	S						

Figure 2

11	C	D	C	D
12	S	C	D	S
13	D	S	H	C
14	S	H	S	D
15	C	C	D	S
16	H	H	C	H
17	H	D	D	S
18	S	S	D	D
19	C	H	S	C
20	D	H	H	H
Score	5	5	7	

Key: C = Club, D = Diamond, H = Heart, S = Spade

When the subject's guess (each guess = 1 trial) corresponds to the actual target card, this is called a hit. You can mark this by circling those boxes on the record sheet. Then enter the total number of hits for the run in the score box.

the cards. Sometimes a subject will prefer to be tested first by the Basic Technique method, feeling that he can score higher if the card he is trying to identify is separated from the rest of the cards. So let us begin by describing the first method (BT).

Get set: Clairvoyance Basic Technique (BT)

1. Select 20 playing cards, 5 of each suit.
2. Prepare record sheets (see Figure 2).
3. The tester and subject sit comfortably at a table.

Go—You're the Tester:

1. Shuffle the cards; be sure the subject does not see the cards being shuffled (go into another room if necessary).
2. Place the deck of 20 cards face down on the table.
3. Remove the top card without looking at it and place it face down on the table.
4. The subject makes his guess.
5. Either the tester or the subject records the guess on the record sheet in the column marked *Call*.
6. The first card is moved to another point on the table without its identity being disclosed.
7. The second target card is taken from the deck and placed separately on the table.
8. The subject makes his guess, this card is placed on top of the first card, etc.
9. After all 20 cards have been guessed, the actual order of the cards themselves is entered on the subject's record sheet by the tester in the column marked *Cards*. (The

card on the bottom of the pile was the subject's first guess.)
10. After the subject has completed 5 runs (5 series of 20 guesses) refer to Table 1.

TABLE 1.

No. of Runs (of 20 trials)	Chance Scores	Good (odds of 20 to 1)	Excellent (odds of 100 to 1)
5	25	34	36
10	50	62	65
15	75	90	93

Suggestion

Use a new or fresh deck of playing cards for each new experiment. A card with any kind of marking offers sensory cues.

Get set: Clairvoyance Down Through the Deck (DT)

1. Select 20 playing cards, 5 of each suit.
2. Prepare record sheets (see Figure 2).
3. Prepare a box or an envelope in which you can enclose the deck of 20 cards. The box or envelope should be small, so that the cards cannot jiggle around and become unshuffled. Playing cards often come in small cardboard boxes; if you have one, that's fine.

Go—You're the Tester:

1. Shuffle the cards; be sure the subject does not see the cards being shuffled (go into another room if necessary).
2. Put the shuffled cards in the box or envelope, then put the box or envelope on a flat surface. The playing cards should be arranged so that they are face down.

3. The subject makes 20 consecutive guesses. He is trying to have his 20 guesses correspond to the order of the 20 cards in the box.
4. Either the subject or the tester records the guesses on the record sheet in the column marked *Call*.
5. When all 20 guesses have been made, the tester removes the cards from the box or envelope, being careful not to disturb the order of the cards.
6. The cards are recorded (beginning with the top card) on the record sheet, in the *Card* column.
7. After the subject has completed 5 runs refer to Table 1 to evaluate the results.

The next test is probably the best one for a restless subject. Here he takes a more active role in the experiment. He actually handles the cards (trying to place each card in its correct position).

Get on your mark—Try this Clairvoyance Four Aces Test:

Get Set:
1. Select a standard deck of 52 playing cards.
2. Prepare record sheets (see Figure 3) and choose a subject.

Go—You're the Tester:
1. Remove the 4 aces and lay them in front of the subject, face up, about 6 inches apart on a flat surface.
2. Shuffle the remaining 48 cards; be sure the subject does not see the cards being shuffled (go into another room if necessary).

No. 1

Name John Smith   Date 10/28

Type of test Clairvoyance - 4 Aces

Suit of Ace	H	S	C	D
	C	S	D	C
	Ⓢ	Ⓢ	H	Ⓗ
	Ⓗ	D	S	D
	D	Ⓢ	Ⓒ	S
	Ⓓ	Ⓢ	C	C
	Ⓗ	Ⓢ	S	Ⓓ
	Ⓗ	C	D	S
	D	H	H	Ⓗ
	C	C	D	Ⓓ
	C	Ⓢ		Ⓓ
	S	D		H
	D	C		S
	Ⓗ	Ⓢ		C
	C	Ⓢ		
		S		
		H		
		C		
Score	4	6	1	4
Total score =	15			

Figure 3.

3. The subject then places each of the 48 cards, one by one, face down, in front of the ace which he believes matches the suit of the card in his hand.
4. When all 48 cards have been placed, turn the 4 piles face up, one pile at a time, and record the number of hits (cards whose suit matches the suit of the ace in front of which they were placed).
5. After the subject has completed the test twice, refer to Table 2 to evaluate the scores.

TABLE 2.

No. of Runs (of 48 trials)	Chance Scores	Good (odds of 20 to 1)	Excellent (odds of 100 to 1)
2	24	32	35
4	48	60	63
8	96	113	118

Suggestions

1. To avoid the subject's falling into any kind of pattern, advise him to take each card as a separate unit, asking himself each time, "What is the suit of this card?"
2. Tell the subject to use any impulse or intuitive feeling which he may have; encourage him to follow the impulse which comes first to mind.
3. Try this test with the aces face down. Although the subject does not know which ace is the club, diamond, heart or spade, he can still use his ESP to put his cards on the right pile. Also, this test eliminates the possibility that the subject is peeking at the cards in

his hand in order to match them properly with the visible aces.

Get on your mark—Try the Precognition Four Aces Test:

Precognition—ESP of the future events—in many ways lends itself to the best kind of test. It eliminates any possibility of sensory cues and it raises some of the most challenging, stimulating and age-old questions about prophets and prophecy, free will and determinism.

Get set:

1. Remove the aces from a standard deck of 52 playing cards and set them aside. With pieces of blank paper mark the places where you wish the subject to make his four piles.
2. Prepare record sheets (see Figure 3).
3. Have on hand a fairly large phone book (at least 100 white pages).

Go:

1. Shuffle the remaining 48 cards thoroughly.
2. The subject, using his precognition, places each card, one by one, in front of the blank marker where he thinks the ace of the same suit will be placed in the future.
3. After all 48 cards have been placed, the position of the aces can be determined. To determine the positions, take the telephone book, close your eyes and open the book at random. Choose the first column on the left-hand page, note the last digit in the first number and use this simple code.

The first ace will be the:
Ace of Clubs if the digit is either   1 or 2
Ace of Diamonds if the digit is either 3 or 4
Ace of Hearts if the digit is either   5 or 6
Ace of Spades if the digit is either   7 or 8
(Ignore the digits 9 and 0)

After you have determined which ace will be the first in line, that is, which ace will replace the first blank marker (from left to right), go on to the next telephone number's last digit to determine (by using the code again) which ace will be the second in the line. If the digit indicates the ace which has already been chosen, ignore that number and go on to the *next* telephone number's last digit. When the positions of the first 3 aces have been determined by this method, put the remaining ace in the fourth position at the end of the line.

4. Turn the piles over one at a time and score them.
5. After the subject has completed the test twice, refer to Table 2 to evaluate the results.

Get on Your Mark—Try the General ESP Test:

Good telepathy tests are very rare. There have only been one or two real telepathy experiments in the history of parapsychology. This is because it is almost impossible to devise a telepathy test. In order to be sure that one is testing for telepathy (and not another type of ESP like clairvoyance or precognition) there can never be any written record of the targets. For example, if a person, the "sender" selects a card from a deck of cards, looks at the card, and concentrates on it, and the "receiver" says, "you are thinking of the seven of diamonds," this may not be telepathy. The receiver may have used clairvoyance to perceive the card itself and not the thoughts of the sender. Many ESP tests allow for the possibility of both telepathy and clairvoyance. These tests, which combine the possibility of mind-to-mind communication and ESP of objects, are called GESP (General ESP) tests.

Two people are involved in a GESP test: the sender (the experimenter can act as the sender), and the subject (or the receiver). The sender tries to communicate a specific thought (such as a name, an object, or an event) to the subject. It is a good idea to work with a fixed set of items such as colors, numbers or cards.

Get Set:
1. Select 20 playing cards, 5 of each suit.
2. Prepare record sheets (see Figure 2).
3. Devise a way to screen the experimenter from the subject, so that visual clues (such as unconscious lip movements of the sender) are not possible. The receiver could simply sit with his back toward the sender. Separate rooms would be better.

Go—You're the Sender:
1. Shuffle the cards; be sure the subject does not see the cards being shuffled (go into another room if necessary).

2. Place the 20 cards, face down, in front of the sender.
3. The sender takes the top card from the deck and says "Ready." He then concentrates on communicating the correct *suit* to the subject. (If clairvoyance were operating, the subject would be more likely to envision the whole card.)
4. The subject records his first guess on the record sheet in the first column marked *Call*. After he has written his guess, the subject says "Next," to indicate to the sender that it is time for him to begin concentrating on the next card.
5. The sender places the first card face down to the right of the other cards (beginning a new pile). He then picks up the next card, says Ready," etc.
6. After all 20 cards have been guessed in this manner, the experimenter enters the actual targets on the subject's record sheet in the first *Card* column. (The first card on the bottom of the pile corresponds to the subject's first guess.)
7. After the subject has completed 5 runs refer to Table 1 to evaluate his score.

Suggestion

If possible, have the sender and the receiver situated in separate rooms, within hearing distance of each other.

These are some of the basic tests for ESP. Although the instructions may seem a bit lengthy and complicated, the tests themselves are simple.

The ABC's of ESP Testing

The role of the ESP tester is a tricky one. You must try to be flexible and change any aspect of the procedure to make an individual subject more relaxed and comfortable. But you must also insist on maintaining certain conditions which control against the possibility of sensory cues (for example, shuffling the cards out of the subject's sight). If you are warm and friendly, your procedure will not seem awkward or restraining; subjects will accept your procedure more willingly and wholeheartedly.

Sometimes you may be tempted to try an impromptu and informal test. For example, you might say to someone, "What am I thinking?" There is no doubt that it would be interesting if someone really did guess what you were thinking. Especially if your thought was one which seemed to be completely out of the ordinary. But where would you go from there? Could you say he had ESP? Wouldn't you want to reserve judgment until you had further tested the individual? A good guess may be indicative of ESP, but good test scores are even better; they can be evaluated statistically as evidence of ESP. Other sciences such as psychology, chemistry and physics also use statistics as their criteria or proof of a phenomenon.

Informal ESP games are popular at parties. Sometimes, although a party group begins with informal "Can you read my mind?" games, people are happy to try something more serious, particularly if you have the testing material handy. Group testing is convenient because it does not take much time, and many guesses or trials are possible. You can easily make your own record sheets; a professional full-page sample is reproduced on page 143.

Children's birthday parties offer excellent opportunities for ESP test games. Children usually respond well to the challenge of a bit of competition and to the promise of reward. You can encourage team competition by comparing the boys' scores with the girls' scores or by having the children choose up sides. Small inexpensive toys or candy could serve as the rewards. At parties, the mood and the spirit are just right, with everyone relaxed, happy, excited and enthusiastically interested in the activities. (For children's tests see Chapter IV.)

If there is in your family or among your friends an invalid who cannot usually participate in competitive games, ESP games might be particularly appealing to him. There is no real evidence as yet to support the idea that people who are deficient or handicapped in some sensory or physical capacity will have a greater amount of ESP to compensate for their deficiency. However, it does seem like a logical possibility, and surely the idea itself might inspire some disabled youngster or oldster to feel that he can outscore his competitors. And indeed he may, since confidence is such an important factor.

ESP is still in many ways an unknown entity. We know that it is "out there," but we can't always find it. It approaches and stays with us for brief snatches of insight and then it disappears again—

without a trace. That is why it is so important to encourage your subjects to follow their hunches, instincts and intuitions; this is how ESP is most likely to make its appearance. That first fleeting impulse, before one is beset by doubts, is a good bet for ESP.

CHAPTER IV

Tests for Children

Children thrive on encouragement and praise. In ESP games children respond to small rewards for high scores with enduring interest and enthusiasm. Here are some gamelike tests which your children may enjoy.

I. WITH MARBLES

Get on your mark: Clairvoyance

Get set:

1. You will need 20 marbles: 4 different colors; 5 of each color.
2. Place the 20 marbles in a paper bag.
3. Prepare a record sheet similar to the one shown in Figure 2 (pp. 32-33).

Go: The object of the game is to have the child guess the color of the unseen marbles.

1. Hold the bag behind your back, shake the bag, then reach in and choose one marble.
2. Keeping the marble concealed, let the child

Tests for Children

guess (only one guess per marble) the color of the marble.
3. Record the guess and the color of the marble.
4. Put the marble back and choose again.
5. Twenty guesses equal one run.
6. Refer to Table 1 (p. 35) to evaluate the scores.

Suggestion: Try offering a bonus marble (or a piece of candy, or a penny, depending on what is most in demand) for 5 hits or more, 2 free marbles for 10 hits or more, 3 free marbles for 15 hits or more and 5 free marbles for a perfect score of 20.

II. WITH CANDY

Get on your mark: Clairvoyance
Get Set:
1. You will need a lot of candy (preferably sour balls wrapped in cellophane). Separate the red candies from the other colors.
2. Put the red candies in one bag, and put the other candies in another bag.
3. Have paper and pencil handy.

Go: The object of the game is to guess the hand which holds the red candy.
1. Choose one candy from each bag.
2. Holding the candies behind your back mix them up until you are no longer sure which candy is which. (If the tester knows which candy is the red candy he may unconsciously tend, say, to extend that hand a bit farther; children can be very sensitive to even a very slight gesture.)
3. Extend your fists in front of you, with one candy in each hand.

4. Have the child point to the hand which he believes holds the red candy.
5. Record both the child's guess and the correct hand (that is, the fist in which the red candy actually was enclosed), and begin again.
6. Ten guesses equal one run.
7. As a bonus you might offer the child the prize of keeping the red candies when he correctly chooses the fist which holds the red candy, or you might offer pennies instead of candy. With older children you could offer a large prize for an above-chance run instead of an immediate reward for each correct guess. So that, perhaps, in a run of 10 guesses:

    6 correct guesses = 1 lollipop
    7 correct guesses = 1 ice cream cup
    8 correct guesses = 1 ice cream cone
    9 correct guesses = 1 ice cream soda
   10 correct guesses = 1 trip to the park
                            or zoo or circus, etc.

8. After 50 guesses or trials (5 runs) refer to Table 3 to evaluate the score.

TABLE 3.

No. of Runs (of 10 trials)	Chance Scores	Good (odds of 20 to 1)	Excellent (odds of 100 to 1)
5	25	32	34
10	50	60	63
20	100	114	118

III. WITH PAPER
Get on your mark: Clairvoyance
Get set:

Tests for Children

1. Have plenty of paper and a pencil handy.
2. Take two pieces of paper (loose-leaf paper, 8x10) and staple them together. Place one sheet directly on top of the other and staple each corner. Repeat 10 times (you will need at least 20 sheets). Two sheets stapled equal one booklet.
3. In the middle of the top sheets mark 5 of the booklets lightly with a check ($\vee$) in pencil. Place a cross (+) lightly and in pencil in the middle of the top sheets of the remaining 5 booklets.
4. Fold each booklet in half so that the paper marked with the check or the cross is on the inside. Now fold the papers in half 3 more times. (If it won't hold together, use a rubber band to keep the folds in place.)
5. Examine the folded booklets to be sure that neither the checks nor crosses are visible.
6. In a paper bag shake the 10 folded booklets. When you think they are thoroughly mixed, take them out of the bag and spread them out.

Go: The object of the game is to select from the 10 folded booklets those booklets which are marked with a check.

1. The subject chooses the 5 folded booklets which he thinks are check booklets.
2. Unfold the 5 booklets and record how many contain checks and how many (if any) contain crosses.
3. Erase all the checks and crosses, mark the 10 top sheets again—with 5 of each mark—

paying no attention to the original marks. This is so that the child will not recognize which booklets have the checks and which booklets have the crosses. Refold these booklets, put all 10 booklets back in the bag, shake, and begin again.

4. After a child has made 50 choices refer to Table 3 to evaluate his score.

Suggestions

1. Once again you may want to offer a small reward for any correct choices, especially in the beginning; but make the rewards more and more promising and enticing for the exceptional score; for instance, a perfect score of 5 checks.

2. This game can be adapted for very young children and babies: spread out the papers on the floor and assume that the first 5 bookets which are touched are the child's choices.

IV. WITH PAPER

Get on your mark: General ESP

Get Set:

1. Follow all the instructions outlined above in III.
2. Place the child in a comfortable chair in one room. The sender (who could be the experimenter) should be seated in another room, close to the first one, with the folded booklets before him.

Go: The object is for the child to identify the symbol (check or cross) which has been chosen.

1. The sender chooses one of the folded booklets, unfolds it and concentrates on "sending" to the subject the symbol (either the check

or the cross) which is marked on the booklet. When he is concentrating he says "Ready."

2. The subject calls out his guess; this is recorded by the sender along with the actual target symbol that the sender concentrated on. The sender chooses another folded booklet and the process is repeated until all 10 booklets have been unfolded.

3. Rewards should be adapted to the situation and the subject. Younger children will find small rewards inspiring while older children may want larger rewards; they may want to be rewarded fairly generously for truly exceptional performances. Determine the criteria and the rewards before the test.

4. After 50 guesses or trials (the game played 5 times) refer to Table 4 to evaluate the results.

TABLE 4.

No. of Runs (of 5 trials)	Chance Scores	Good (odds of 20 to 1)	Excellent (odds of 100 to 1)
4	5	9	10
8	10	15	16
12	15	22	24

V. WITH SUPERMAN

Get on your mark: Precognition

Get set—Draw up this simple game:

1. Superman is in disguise. Which man do you think is really Superman?

52 TEST YOUR ESP

2. Superman is looking for Lois Lane. Which house do you think she is in?

3. Superman must make a phone call but one of the phones contains the ingredient which is deadly to him, Kryptonite. Which phone do you think contains Kryptonite?

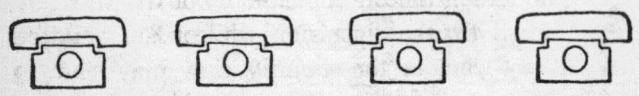

4. The jewel thieves have hidden the stolen jewels in one of these boxes. Which box do you think contains the stolen jewels?

5. Superman must return as quickly as possible to the *Daily Planet* building where he works (disguised as mild-mannered reporter, Clark Kent). Which sign do you think offers the shortest route?

Go:
1. Each subject takes the test either by reading it or by having it read to him. The subject's answer, always a number, 1 through 4, is written on a separate piece of paper.

2. To determine the correct answers you will need a telephone book (one with at least 100 white pages). Close your eyes and open the book at random. Choose the first column on the left-hand page, note the last digit in the first number and use this simple code:

The answer to the first question will be:

1 if the digit is either 1 or 2
2 if the digit is either 3 or 4
3 if the digit is either 5 or 6
4 if the digit is either 7 or 8
(Ignore the digits 9 and 0)

Take the second number in the same column in the telephone book, note the last digit in this number and use this digit to determine the answer to the second question. Continue this procedure with the next 3 numbers' last digits, and determine the answers to the remaining questions.

3. If you play the game again with the same subject explain that the answers will probably be different each time he plays. So, for each game he must be prepared to use fresh insight or ESP.

4. Choose a new page in the telephone book each time the game is played.

5. After 20 guesses or trials (4 games) refer to Table 4 to evaluate the scores.

All of us, children as well as adults, have our individual differences. It is important to keep this in mind when testing for ESP. Try to accept each child for the individual he is and try to make him feel comfortable and at home with your testing situation. To maintain peaceful and relaxing conditions, offer the children whatever comforts you think they may want. This could range from a cool drink to a lollipop.

Some children find it difficult to concentrate on anything for long periods of time. For those children who cannot concentrate for more than a few minutes at a time, you can arrange many short tests or testing sessions, rather than one or two long ones. Also, continue to introduce new elements into the tests or games by varying the procedures and by gradually offering more enticing rewards.

If you treat your subjects with respect, they will respect you and your tests. From what parapsychologists have seen of ESP, friendship and trust seem to be practically inspirational. If possible, even members of your family should be treated as honored guests when they are your subjects.

CHAPTER V

Testing with Photographs

As you know by now, an ESP test can be devised by using practically anything at hand. Any items from bridge cards and ESP cards to chewing gum and candy offer opportunities for devising tests of your own, mainly for either clairvoyance or precognition.

Such objects—and especially the standard deck of ESP cards—have proved time and again to be excellent stimuli for exercising your ESP in a way that will give results which can be evaluated statistically.

One of the major complaints made by mediums who have been tested using the ESP deck, is that they are unable to get any feeling about the cards. You may have some of your subjects express the same opinion: that is, that there is not an emotional link between themselves and the cards. A subject who has this feeling has a psychological barrier that you must both overcome before he can perform at his best. Rather than try to reason with him and convince him that this emotional linkage is not necessary, it is much easier to adapt the testing situation to *his* needs. You could hide one of a couple of people behind a door and ask the subject to guess which one is there; but, unfortunately, here you would run into various difficulties in establishing that ESP was really responsible for correct guesses, even if the answers were 100 per cent correct. Sensory cues could not possibly be ruled out in such an experiment because the person making the guesses may perceive (even subliminally) clues to the hiding person's identity. Perfume, the smell of tobacco, even the way a person breathes —all could give clues which would lead to a correct guess through sensory means only.

There is, however, an ideal situation which eliminates such sensory cues and yet establishes an "emotional relationship" for the subject. This involves the use of photographs instead of the ESP cards or other "barren" stimuli. The subject can even supply the photographs himself, of people with whom he has a close attachment or a deep and meaningful relationship (or whom he hates). This should help to overcome his feeling that the test objects are meaningless. By overcoming this initial psychological block, the subject may become more relaxed and more receptive to the testing situation.

Dr. Katherine M. Banham, a psychologist at Duke University, recently conducted two ESP tests using photographs. Her tests consisted of two aspects: sex and emotion. Twelve photographs

Testing with Photographs

were used, three of smiling males, 3 of unsmiling males, 3 of smiling females, and 3 of unsmiling females. Each photograph was enclosed in an opaque envelope. The 12 envelopes were shuffled together much like a small deck of cards and presented to the subject. Holding the "deck" in his hands, the subject then looked at the top envelope and tried to guess whether it contained a photo of a male or of a female and whether the person in the photograph was happy or unhappy. By chance alone, using the 12 photos, the subject was expected to guess 6 correctly for the sex aspect and 6 for the emotion aspect.

You will probably want to make your own experimental research with photos less elaborate and easier to deal with. The method to be used is simple. Have the subject wait in another room where there is no chance of his observing you. Twelve photographs will be needed: 6 of males and 6 of females. Studio photographs are not necessary; the simple snapshots which are usually available in any home are adequate, as long as there is only one person in each picture and it is clearly discernible that the person is male or female. (In other words, a hazy photograph of a girl in slacks, or an unclear shot of a young man with long hair and beads would not be ideal.) It is important to use the same size photographs, as the outline of the size could possibly give a clue as to which photograph is being used.

After selecting your 12 photographs of the same size, arrange them in a single row down the center of a table. Use an opaque tablecloth to cover the photos. Double check to see that there is no way by which the subject can see through the cloth. You are now ready for your subject to begin making his guesses.

It is a good idea to use the same sequence for guessing in each run (that is, for each time the subject guesses the 12 photos). If you begin with the subject guessing from the left to the right, then all other runs during the session should be done in the same order. The reason for this is that it keeps instructions to a minimum; also, the subject will not be as apt to be confused by having to call differently for each run.

Explain to the subject that he is to make only one guess regarding the sex of the person in each photo. Be sure to record "male" or "female" as he makes his guess for each of the 12. Then remove the table cloth and record the order of the pictures, checking to see which guesses were correct.

After this has been done, send the subject back into the other room and shuffle the 12 pictures, arrange them in a new single row and cover them again. The subject is then called back to make his guesses again. This process is repeated until the subject has been tested 10 times. Since there are only 2 possible answers, you will expect to average 6 correct answers per run if chance alone is operating. This means that in 10 runs, by chance alone, your subject will get only 60 "hits" or correct guesses. Any scores above this number are probably indicative of ESP in operation. To see to what degree this is (or what the odds against chance would be) look at Table 5 given below. Since some subjects may be interested in trying more than 10 runs, the table is arranged for varying numbers of runs, so that you may be able to give a series of tests of 10 runs per series. It is recommended that short sessions be held as more than 10 runs at a time may tire a subject, resulting in a tendency to do less well. If you wish to test a subject 50 times, then it is best to test him for 10 runs on 5 different occasions.

TABLE 5.

No. of Runs (of 12 trials each)	Chance Scores	Good (odds of 20 to 1)	Excellent (odds of 100 to 1)
10	60	73	78
20	120	144	152
30	180	215	222
40	240	286	295
50	300	356	365

CHAPTER VI

Test Your Pet

From time to time one hears stories of strange, almost unbelievable animal behavior. These incidents, if reported accurately, involve knowledge that came to the animal in some way that did not involve the use of its physical senses. There is no apparent explanation for them—except ESP.

The study of ESP in animals, called *anpsi* (short for *ani*mal *psi*), is relatively new. It began in the early 1920's when a Russian neurophysiologist, Dr. W. Bechterev, published a report of his experiments in telepathically influencing the behavior of a dog. Dr. Bechterev and his assistants placed several objects around a room and concentrated on the one they wished Pikki, a fox terrier, to bring to them. The dog usually brought the correct object.

Shortly after this, Drs. J. B. and L. E. Rhine investigated reports of a horse, Lady, who answered questions asked of her by pointing with her hoof to lettered blocks. They conducted two series of experiments with the mare, and concluded that the best explanation for some of her behavior appeared to be that she was responding to her mistress' thoughts.

Very little anpsi experimenting has taken place since this pioneer work showed that extrasensory communication might take place between people and animals. Anpsi that was independent of human influences needed to be studied. An experiment needed to be designed in which an animal could be tested for its own extrasensory perception in the laboratory. This proved to be extremely difficult.

The physical problems of constructing mazes and eliminating odors from food targets that the animal was to find, etc., were time consuming and troublesome. But the real stumbling block to anpsi in the laboratory proved to be the presence of a human experimenter who knew the location of the target and how the animal could get to it. The experimenter's knowledge of the target's location could influence the animal's behavior whether or not the experimenter was conscious of his own thoughts.

A method had to be found whereby the location of targets could be determined at random by a machine which would then set up the experiment and record whether the response the animal made was correct or not. Recently, this has been done in France, and the results of the experimenting so far look good.

Meanwhile, in 1950, the staff of the Duke University Parapsychology Laboratory began a survey of unexplained animal behavior that suggested possible anpsi. It was hoped that studying anpsi in life situations would help parapsychologists design better experiments with which to test it in the laboratory.

Members of the staff began to collect and organize reports of people who had had unusual experiences with their animals. The reports came from all over the world, and many different animal species were described.

Then, a rather serious problem had to be dealt with, that of possible errors in reporting. People could report their impressions of what an animal had seen or felt and how it had acted, but even the best of these reports was second-hand information. What criteria could be used to evaluate these cases?

The answer was apparent very quickly, because an overwhelming number of the reports had similar features. Animals, distant from each other had exhibited similar reactions to similar situations. From these similarities, generalizations could be made that, in effect, might cancel out mistakes in individual memory and observation.

Many of the cases were investigated; from an acquaintance with people whose animals had had these experiences, it was sometimes possible to tell whether a hoax had been intended or not. Most people interviewed seemed sincere; many were even a little embarrassed, knowing how incredible their claims must seem.

From the cases studied, 6 categories of behavior involving possible anpsi emerged: (1) Psi Trailing, (2) Death Reactions, (3) Reactions to Impending

Danger, (4) Homing, (5) Awareness of Approach and (6) Miscellaneous Behavior, suggesting telepathy.

(1) Psi Trailing

This category most clearly suggests anpsi. In these cases, an animal separated from a person or a mate to whom it had been attached followed the one it loved into wholly unfamiliar territory. The trip sometimes took several weeks to over a year, depending on the distance involved, and the animal usually arrived bedraggled and footsore from its journey. Perhaps someday we will know what guided these animals in the right direction, in spite of the hardships and the many miles, under conditions in which no conceivable sensory trail was possible.

A physical deformity played an important role in the identification of a cat who came from California to find its family in Oklahoma.

When the S.W. family left northern California for Gage, Oklahoma, they decided to give their cat, Sugar, to neighbors who had his littermate, Spice. Two weeks later Sugar disappeared from his new home. The neighbors thought it best not to mention the matter to the W. family, who by that time were busy getting settled on their new ranch 1,500 miles away.

Fourteen months later, Mrs. W. was standing

near an open window in her new barn when a large cat jumped from the window sill onto her shoulder. The cat began to purr and to rub itself against Mrs. W.'s neck. Mrs. W. was startled and brushed the cat to the ground. She noticed the cat was very similar to Sugar in such externals as color and size.

"Sugar has come to visit us," she called to her husband. They both laughed, for neither of them believed it could possibly be Sugar.

The cat showed special attention to Mrs. W. just as Sugar had done in California. Later, as Mrs. W. stroked the cat, she felt a horny protuberance on the animal's lower back.

"Why this *is* Sugar," she exclaimed.

Sugar had had a deformity in the lower region of his back when he was given to the W.'s.

Some months later, the California neighbors with whom Sugar had been left paid a visit to the W. ranch.

"What is Sugar doing here?" remarked the wife. She felt for the protuberance on his back, and told of the cat's departure from her home over a year before. Now there seemed to be no doubt that Sugar had really found the way to his family in Oklahoma.

A similarly curious case was reported in a Massachusetts newspaper. The death of a farmer brought his pets to his graveside on the day of his funeral. This was alarming to some of the other mourners who had come to pay him their respects, for his pets were bees.

During his life Mr. Z. had raised, worked with,

and loved bees. When he died, his friends and family gathered at the cemetery for funeral services. As his cortege reached the grave, mourners found the funeral tent covered with bees. They did not annoy anyone but remained immobile, covering the tent ceiling and clinging to floral sprays.

(A hundred years ago, it was customary to "tell" bees of a death in the family by draping their hives in black crepe. Otherwise it was thought that the bees might leave in search of a new home.)

(2) Death Reactions

Most perplexing among the anpsi cases are the Death Reactions. An animal may show what appears to be a reaction to the unknown death or approaching death of its master or someone else, or it may react to premonitions of its own death.

The animal, most frequently a dog, will exhibit behavior for which there seems no apparent reason at the time it happens. It may whine or cry or howl or persistently try to get the attention of a human acquaintance as if to tell him that something is wrong, or it may ignore attention that it is given and mope.

Many cases involving a dog's howl, apparently signaling death or approaching death, have been reported. One of the earliest recorded references to this phenomenon was made by a sixteenth-century writer who noted that "dogs by their howling portend death and calamities." In the 1800's, another author wrote that "a dog's distressful howling presages death especially in houses where someone is lying ill."

(3) Reactions to Impending Danger

Very similar to Death Reactions are Reactions to Impending Danger. Again, the animal exhibits behavior which at the time seems unexplainable.

The danger involved may be to the animal's master, or to someone it knows, or to the animal itself. In the former cases, the animals are, again, usually dogs and, in the latter cases, the danger is often from a natural disaster and the animals involved are of many species.

Mrs. F.G. of Amsterdam, New York, reported an incident in which her husband's dog may have saved her life.

Bob was Mr. G.'s pet bulldog and his constant companion. One morning, when Mr. G. started for work, the dog refused to go along with him as was his custom. When Bob did not respond to whistling or coaxing, Mr. G. thought that perhaps the dog felt sick and did not try again to persuade him to leave the house. The dog settled himself on the davenport by the door and Mrs. G. began to do the dishes. An hour passed, and suddenly Bob, in the next room, began to bark furiously. Mrs. G. went into the dining room to see why the dog was barking, and there stood a large menacing-looking man. He did not speak but came toward her. Bob approached him, growling and barking.

"If you come one step closer," Mrs. G. told the man, "this dog will tear you apart. I am going upstairs to call the police."

Mrs. G. ran upstairs while Bob kept the man at bay. As Mrs. G. reached for the telephone, she saw the man run from the yard and decided not to call for help.

At noon when Mr. G. came to lunch he asked how Bob had been.

"Bob has been fine," said Mrs. G. "This morning he helped me a great deal."

The central California earthquake of 1925 did much damage in the Santa Barbara area. High buildings collapsed, and low-lying lands were flooded. Several days before the quake, Miss J.H. of Atascadero, California, near Santa Barbara, noticed her cat moving its kittens. The kittens had been under a manger used for storage in the barn. The mother cat was moving them to an unsteady looking box not far away which was about 5 feet above ground level. Miss N. thought this was strange, for the cat had seemed happy under the manger.

Later that week, the earthquake released a wall of water which flooded Miss H.'s barn, among other areas; the kittens, now above the water level, were not harmed.

(4) Homing

No one knows the range of the physical senses in nonhuman species. For example, recent experiments show that a salmon's sense of smell is so keen that it is able to identify the stream of its birth by its odor, and literally smells its way home from the sea to spawn. Homing instincts like that of the salmon are common to many living species. Thus far, too few studies have been done to determine what guides most species unerringly toward home. It may be that ESP is involved. Mr. G.B. of Silverton, Oregon, had an experience with his dog, Bobbie, which strongly suggests that in some cases, at least, it is.

Bobbie, a large collie, was lost in Wolcott, Indiana, when the B. family was making a trip east from Oregon. The B.s delayed their trip several days to find the dog, but neither their inquiries nor a newspaper advertisement brought any news of Bobbie.

Unable to stay longer in Indiana, the B.s continued their trip to Florida and then returned to Oregon.

Six months later, Bobbie came home. His feet were in such bad condition that he did not walk again for three days. No one had any doubts about Bobbie's identity. Three of his teeth had been missing, there was a prominent scar over his right eye and a tractor had run over him as a puppy and thrown his hips out of line. These features, along with his breed markings and unusual size, left little doubt that Bobbie had found his way home to Oregon.

The Oregon Humane Society publicized the story of Bobbie's travels, and many people who had befriended Bobbie on his way home wrote to the B.s. Through this correspondence, Bobbie's route home was roughly traced. He had gone southwest and then north, a route very different from the northern one over which the B.s had taken him to Indiana.

(5) Awareness of Approach

Often an animal is aware of the time of day its master returns home from work, if he does so regularly. Many dogs—and sometimes cats—will take a certain position by the door or by the front gate or driveway, or they may awaken and seem restless, staying in the vicinity of the door by which their master will enter the house.

Sometimes when the master returns unexpectedly, the animal seems to know about it beforehand, too. Incidents like the following one are not unusual.

When J.H. of Liverpool, England, was a mining apprentice near Durham, he bought a bull terrier puppy which he trained from the age of about 6 weeks. When the dog was a little over a year old,

Mr. H. began to leave her with his landlady in Ferryhill when he went home to Whetby for weekends. He usually went by bus on Saturday and returned on Sunday or Monday, the times of his return varying considerably.

One weekend in December, he went home, leaving the dog, as usual with the landlady and telling her that he would return the following Monday afternoon. Snow began to fall on the moors, and he decided to return Sunday evening instead. He was unable to send a message to his landlady.

When he arrived in Ferryhill at about 7:00 p.m., he found his supper ready for him. His landlady expressed no surprise at his coming. She told him that his dog would always go to sit by the front door about half an hour before his return and stay there until he came home.

An animal may show anticipatory behavior for a longer period of time before its master's return, if the master's absence has been a long one. Mrs. R.L.C. of San Angelo, Texas, reported such a case.

Danny, the family's dog, had been in the habit of waiting at a certain spot in the road for about half an hour before Mrs. C.'s youngest brother came home from school each evening. One summer the boy went to a relative's farm 300 miles away to help during the harvests. He stayed there most of the summer, writing infrequently and naming no specific date for his return.

One afternoon in August, Danny took his accustomed waiting position in the road. No one could induce him to leave it. A few hours later, along came the brother, suitcase in hand, walking down the road. He had taken advantage of an unexpected chance to get a ride home.

(6) Miscellaneous Cases Suggesting Possible Telepathy

These miscellaneous cases deal with no specific situation but suggest from the behavior of the animal involved that it is responding to its master's thoughts or wishes. Mrs. B.M.S. of Upper Darby, Pennsylvania, recorded one such case. She thought of her dog Skippy on several occasions when she opened the refrigerator and noticed some table scraps he would like. As she thought of him, she would hear the scamper of his feet on the stairs as he rushed down to the kitchen. Mrs. S. decided that Skippy probably heard the refrigerator door opening and that the sound suggested to him the possibility of a handout. Without making a sound she tried simply thinking of something to give him. As soon as her mind dwelt on that subject, Skippy would come running to her; he would then sit and beg for a tidbit that was not yet visible.

Testing

There are several simple ESP tests which can be given to your dog or cat.

Object Test

If your pet has been trained to fetch an object, try this one. Throw out two objects of a similar size and appearance at the same time. You should throw them in the same direction so that they land fairly close together. One method of doing this is to tie them together. If this is done, the objects must be tied in such a way that the dangling object will not hinder the animal when he is bringing the one he has chosen. Two balls or sticks, tied a few inches apart, may do it.

The objects should be marked or colored in some way so as to be easily distinguishable when they are thrown some distance away. You must choose which of the two objects you wish your animal to bring, and concentrate on that one. When your animal is successful, reward him.

Your pet has a 50-50 chance of bringing the object you have chosen. You may want to keep a record of the number of times you test him and what percentage of the time he chooses the correct object. If you test him 30 times and he is correct 15 times, his performance is just what would be expected by chance. If, however, he is correct 20 or 25 times, then he is doing very well.

Feedpan Test

At mealtime you might put out two feedpans instead of one for your dog or cat. The feedpans should be located so that they are equally convenient to the animal. They can be placed 6 to 8 inches apart. Both should contain the same amount of food. (Avoid using a feedpan the animal is used to along with one he is unfamiliar with, since this, rather than ESP, may determine his choice.) Pick the dish you wish the animal to eat from and concentrate on it.

Here, as in the object test, the animal has a 50 per cent chance of choosing correctly. By chance, he should choose correctly half of the time. You may want to keep a record of his responses over several weeks, as above, to determine how well he has done.

Anticipatory Behavior Test

Earlier we discussed animal behavior which suggested anticipation of the master's return. We indicated that this behavior may be your pet's response to your usual pattern, if you arrive home regularly at a certain time of day. By varying your time of return by half an hour to an hour, if possible, and by changing the vehicle in which you ride, you can make a good test. If your pet is waiting to meet you as before, or if a member of your family reports that your dog or cat has still shown its accustomed anticipatory behavior, it may really be due to ESP.

Suggestions

In all tests with pets you must be careful not to give clues to the animals. For example, if you are trying the Feedpan Test, since you are concentrating on the pan you wish the animal to select you might unconsciously lean to one side, look at one of the two dishes, etc. Similar hints can arise in the Object Test also. One way around these hindrances to objectivity is for you to select the dish and concentrate while in another room, and have someone who doesn't know which dish is the target bring your pet into the room and subsequently tell you which dish the pet chose. Here, if the animal does well, we can be more certain that it was due to ESP.

CHAPTER VII

Yes, There Is "Negative" ESP

By now you have perhaps tested your husband, children, neighbor and possibly even Fido. If you followed instructions you probably have some interesting results and are wondering, "What now?" Before we discuss what your next step might be, let's mention one thing we have not discussed, but should.

In your testing you have probably obtained some results which were considerably above chance. It is easy to explain why those people you tested scored above chance—they used their ESP. You may also have run into some results which puzzle you; some people have scored considerably *below* chance! This, too, requires an explanation, but it is not as easy to understand as is high scoring.

An analogy may help. Let's imagine you are taking a history test in which there are 100 true-or-false questions. There is only one problem: the

75

test you are taking is written in a foreign language you do not know. However, you decide to check off your 100 answers anyway. Because there are only two possible answers to each question, you have a 50-50 chance of getting each question correct. Thus, even though you can't understand the questions, you can expect to get approximately 50 answers correct. If, when your paper is returned, you discover that you failed to answer even a single question correctly, you would no doubt wonder what caused such a curious score. In the early days of ESP research, parapsychologists found themselves in a somewhat similar situation.

When they began testing, they discovered several high-scoring subjects, and this was fine—it showed that they had ESP. However, they also discovered that some people scored consistently below chance. For a while there was no explanation for this odd phenomenon. Now, however, it is realized that low scoring is just as much an indication of ESP as is high scoring. It would seem that in order to give the wrong answer almost always (say, on a true-or-false test), it is necessary to know the correct answers. The same is true on an ESP test. Those people who score below chance use their ESP to perceive what the correct answer is subconsciously, but for some reason they block out this answer and give an incorrect one. These low scorers do not realize what is happening; they may think they are trying to do their best, just like everyone else, but they block out the correct answer. As to the analogy with the history test in a foreign languge, we may assume that you knew more of the language than

Yes, There Is "Negative" ESP 77

you realized, and, for some reason, did not really want to succeed.

Now that we have seen that low scoring is just as much evidence of ESP as is high scoring, you will want to be on the lookout for it in your tests, if you have not already noticed it. Low scoring *and* high scoring are both more significant than are chance scores. The way to see what the odds are for a given set of low scores is precisely the same as for a set of high scores. For example, in Table 1 (p. 35) we saw that to obtain odds of 100 to 1 for high scoring, out of 100 trials we need 36 hits, 11 hits above the 25 expected by chance. To obtain odds of 100 to 1 from low scoring, 11 hits *below* chance is needed, for a total score of 14. Thus, all the tables in the earlier chapters can also be used to evaluate low scoring.

You may be asking yourself "why do some people block out the correct answers and others not?" This is a question to which there are many answers. Early in ESP research it was discovered that people who "believe in ESP" tend to score higher than people who do not. Those who are skeptical about ESP are frequently those who score below chance. This fact was established in an interesting way.

When subjects were being tested for ESP, they were given questionnaires to fill out, similar to Figure 4 below.

Figure 4.

Name_____

1. Have you ever had a hunch that something you had lost was in a particular, but very unlikely, place—and, in fact, it was?
   Yes   No

2. Have you ever had a dream that later came true?
   Yes   No

3. Have you ever had a hunch that a particular person would have a serious illness or accident which later actually happened as you anticipated?
   Yes   No

4. Did you ever know in advance that you were going to receive a phone call from a particular person on a particular day, when you really had no way of knowing this?
   Yes   No

5. Do you consider yourself lucky in whatever you do?
   Yes   No

As you can see, the questions are designed to see what a person's attitude toward ESP is. If he

Yes, There Is "Negative" ESP

answers "No" to most of the questions he is probably skeptical. If he answers "Yes" he is probably favorably disposed to the idea of ESP.

After the early subjects filled out the questionnaire, they took ESP tests. Then on the basis of their answers to the questionnaire, they were divided into two groups: believers and nonbelievers. The scoring rates of these two groups were compared and it was found that the rate for the believers was considerably higher than that for the nonbelievers. You may want to see this effect for yourself. Here's an advanced experiment you can try.

Make 10 copies of the questionnaire in Figure 4 and give them to 10 friends to fill out. Give 5 to friends who you are pretty sure are skeptical and 5 to friends whom you'd classify as believers. Then give each friend 2 runs of the Four Aces Test which was described in Chapter III. Now, take the tests of those 5 who answered "Yes" to at least 3 of the questions and add the results. By chance you would expect a total of 120 hits. Since these are the believers we would expect their ESP to cause high scores. Now take the tests of the remaining 5 (the nonbelievers) and add their scores. Here we expect to find fewer hits than one would expect by chance. In order to see if the two groups really did score differently, you must find the total difference. For example, let's say that the believers' scores totalled 131, which is 11 above chance. Let's also assume that the nonbelievers scored 102, which is 18 below chance. In all, the difference in scoring is 29. (11

+ 18) To see the odds against chance we refer to Table 6. From Table 6 we can see that the odds are greater than 20 to 1 against such a large difference happening through chance alone.

Table 6.

Difference in Scoring	Odds
27	20 to 1 (Good)
34	100 to 1 (Excellent)

We mentioned earlier that there are many answers to the question, "Why do some people block out the correct answers and others not?" We have seen that one factor is attitude toward ESP, and have even outlined an experiment to demonstrate this. Another factor which can cause low scoring is poor testing conditions. Also, if the person tested is tired, in a bad mood, rushed, etc., this, too, can cause low scoring.

People may never change their basic attitudes toward ESP, but they certainly do change their moods. For this reason the same person may score above chance one day and below chance another day. You may want to see for yourself just what effect mood has on ESP scores. Because you can judge your mood better than you can judge someone else's, you can test yourself in this simple experiment.

Using the Four Aces Test, test yourself 10 times when you are in a particularly good mood. Also test yourself 10 times when you feel yourself to be tired, irritable, etc. You do not have to do all 10 runs in one mood before you test yourself in the other mood. Rather, mix the runs as they come, but be

Yes, There Is "Negative" ESP

sure to indicate on your record sheet in what mood you were when you took the test.

In the end, you should have 20 runs; 10 done when you were cheerful, rested, etc., and 10 when you were in a bad mood. Once again, see how many above chance (chance is 120 for each condition) you did on the 10 good-mood tests and how many below on the 10 bad-mood tests. Add the two deviations from chance to get your total difference. You can then use Table 6 to evaluate your results.

The two tests we have described in this chapter are called "Differential Experiments," because the person or persons being tested are expected to react "differentially," or differently, to two different test situations. In the first case, people with positive attitudes are expected to score differently than people with negative attitudes toward ESP; in the second case the same person is expected to score differently according to whether he is in a bad mood or a good mood. The two tests are somewhat advanced, but you may find them extremely rewarding.

One thing to remember when evaluating differential tests is that you can add the deviation from chance of one condition to the deviation from chance of the other condition *only* when one condition gave *above*-chance scoring and the other gave *below*-chance scoring. If you should find, for example, that both test conditions gave above-chance scoring, then you cannot add the two deviations. Rather, you must *subtract* the smaller deviation from the larger. This is logical, since you want the *difference* between the two. If one condition say, gives 20 hits above chance and the other 5 hits above chance, then the difference is only 15 and not 25.

CHAPTER VIII

Party Games with ESP

It is interesting to note that there is no good evidence of group ESP occurring in everyday life. There are, of course, numerous examples of individuals, or even two persons, becoming spontaneously aware (through ESP) of some distant event. There is, however, no recorded instance of a group of people all becoming aware of something by ESP. This is most curious since there doesn't seem to be any reason why an entire group could not spontaneously exhibit ESP.

Parapsychologists, when they perform their experiments, often test entire groups, and have discovered in this way considerable evidence for ESP. There are several reasons why parapsychologists test groups. The most important is that it is a way of collecting many guesses very quickly. Imagine if you wanted to do an experiment in which you needed 10,000 guesses and you had to obtain them by individual testing! However, if you had just given a lecture on ESP to 100 people and had them all together, this might be the ideal time to collect your 10,000 guesses; just ask each person to make 100 guesses. When figuring out the odds for the results of your experiment, it is statistically the same whether you have 100 people make 100 guesses each or one person make 10,000 guesses (poor fellow). In this chapter, we will not suggest that you test one person 10,000 times, nor will we tell you how to test 100 people at once. But you might find it fun to try some ESP games at your next party or gathering. Aside from having a great deal of fun, you might get some interesting results. Before we describe some of the games you can try, it might be well to point out one of the advantages of testing in a party atmosphere.

In the short history of parapsychology, there have been several perfect scores with the standard ESP deck. That is, the person tested guessed correctly all 25 cards. The story behind one of these perfect performances will illustrate our point. You will remember that one of the first high-scoring subjects was Hubert Pearce, a divinity student at Duke University. After Pearce had been tested for a considerable period of time, he became bored and Dr. J. B. Rhine, the experimenter, had difficulty interesting Pearce in the experiment. This was during the depression, when money was tight, and Rhine decided to try offering a huge reward to stimulate his subject. One day he said to Pearce, "I'll give you $100 for every card you get correct." It was clear, then, that the subject's interest was aroused. The guessing began. At the end of the test, Pearce, almost exhausted from the strain, said "You'll never get me to do that again." He had gotten all 25 correct. The point is that when you challenge your subject and arouse him, you may get exceptional results.

At a party you may be able to create such a challenging situation. Some people will react to competition. If you form teams, those with a high competitive spirit may excel and, ideally, reveal their ESP. There are those who like the limelight, and they, too, may score quite well when asked to perform. For these reasons, and many more, don't be surprised if you discover a high-scoring subject at your next party.

Now we can begin to outline some games which we think you and your friends will enjoy.

An ESP Bee

This is a game which will be fun for all, but especially those people who enjoy competition on an individual basis. The procedure is similar to that of a spelling bee.

The players stand and line up around the room. The tester takes a standard deck of playing cards and shuffles them thoroughly. He then selects a card from the deck and asks the first person to guess what the color of the card is, red or black. (The tester must, of course, be careful to hide the card from the players—a small screen would be useful.) If the player successfully guesses the card, he remains standing; if he is wrong, he sits down. The play continues to the first player's left. The tester places the selected card back in the deck and shuffles the cards again. The second player then gets his chance as did the first player. The object of the game is to remain standing by guessing the cards correctly. The last person to remain standing is the winner.

One important detail that must not be overlooked is that after each guess the isolated card must be returned to the deck. This is so that each time the player makes a guess his chances at being correct are 50-50. If the cards were not replaced, there would be a problem. If on the first 5 turns all 5 cards were black, and they were not placed back in the deck, then the sixth player would know that most of the remaining cards were red. Thus his correct guess might not be due to ESP. If you replace the card each time before you shuffle, then this likelihood cannot arise.

Another aspect which is important is the recording of results. It will be best if you try to keep a party spirit going and not turn your game into a stuffy experiment, slowed down by a complicated recording procedure. You might even not tell the players that you are keeping score. What you can do is just jot down on a piece of paper a √ for each hit and an × for each miss. This will not take much time and will be sufficient. After the game is over you can pleasantly surprise your guests by telling them you have been keeping score and that you can tell them the odds against their

Party Games with ESP

ESP performance being due to chance. To do this you can use the table below. Because of the way the game is played, you will not be able to stop play after a given number of guesses. Consequently, the table below may not contain the exact number of guesses in your game. To get an idea of the odds, though, you can look at the number of guesses in the table closest to the actual number of guesses in your game.

TABLE 7

Number of Guesses	Good (odds of 20 to 1)	Excellent (odds of 100 to 1)
20	15	16
25	18	19
30	21	22
40	26	28
50	32	34
60	38	40

Follow-up and a Variation on the ESP Bee

After your game is over and you have a winner, you might ask him for a demonstration. By now his confidence should be high and he might enjoy being given more of the spotlight. What you can do here is just ask him to make a series of 20 guesses in the same manner as in the game he just won. He should feel at home with this technique. When he has finished his 20 guesses, you can use Table 7 to tell him how well he did.

In the ESP Bee described above, the players are asked to guess the color of the card. Thus, by chance they should be correct half the time; the idea is to be correct more than just 50 per cent of the time. But, even by chance alone players are likely to be right at least half of the time, and this gives them a feeling of success which is desirable. However, after you have tried the ESP Bee once, you may want to try a slight variation which will really challenge the players. This variation can also be used if you have a very large number of players and a faster game is needed.

In this variation, everything is the same except that rather than guess the color of a playing card, the player attempts to guess the suit of the card. Here he has a one-in-four chance of being correct rather than a one-in-two chance. Consequently, if chance alone is operating, the players as a group should get not 50 per cent hits, but only 25 per cent. This will cause players to be seated more quickly, and the game will be faster moving. To evaluate the results of this variation, use Table 8.

TABLE 8

Number of Guesses	Good (odds of 20 to 1)	Excellent (odds of 100 to 1)
10	5	6
15	7	8
20	9	10
25	11	12
30	12	13
40	15	17

Putting Your Heads Together

The ESP Bee should appeal to individualists; here is a party game which is designed to rouse everyone's team spirit and should interest those who prefer not to stand out in a crowd.

Divide the players into two teams. To heighten the competition you can have the men against the women; oldsters against youngsters; etc. The only advance preparation you will need is to have a shuffled deck of playing cards face down in its box.

Each team's objective is to guess the *suits* of the top 20 cards in the deck. Each team is to come up with one set of 20 guesses. Thus, the members of a team must put their heads together and make a community decision on each card. This decision can be made in two ways. You can supply each player with a piece of paper and all the members can write down their guesses for the 20 cards, from top to bottom. Then they can see how many votes there were for each suit for the first card, the second card, etc. The suit receiving the most votes (guesses) is the group's guess for that card. After the guesses for all 20 cards have been decided, you can check up and see how well both teams did. Naturally, the team with the most correct guesses wins.

There is a second way of arriving at the community vote which may be more fun for the players than writing down individual guesses and taking the majority's vote. Each team can arrive at a decision through discussion of each card. In this case, if one person has a strong hunch for a particular card, the group can decide to take that hunch as their guess. Thus, by discussing how strong their hunches are, the members of a team can arrive at their guesses for the 20 cards. It will be fun especially if two players both have strong but different hunches about the same card. Since the team can use only one of the hunches, it will be fun to see who was right. If you want to evaluate the results and see how well either team did, you can look at the 20-guess section of Table 8.

For variety you can have the players guess fewer or more than 20 cards, whichever best suits the mood. (You can still use Table 8 to evaluate your results.)

If you play this game more than once with the same teams, you may find that one team consistently beats the other. This may indicate that the better ESP subjects are all on one team. To even things up, you can handicap the better team one or two correct guesses. You could rearrange the teams, but it might prove especially interesting to see if the same team continues to win even under a handicap.

We feel that the party games we have described here will be fun for all, and that's important. If, for some reason the players' interest level is dropping, then chances are that scores will drop too and it is

Party Games with ESP 91

time to stop. Throughout these games, a gay and happy mood should prevail. Don't be surprised if you find some high scores, but most important, have a good time at it.

CHAPTER IX

Mind Over Matter

So far we have only been concerned with ESP; there is still another, perhaps even more amazing, aspect to man's psychic abilities. Mind over matter—the ability of the mind to move and influence objects directly—is quite different from ESP. In the case of ESP, a person, somehow, without the use of his senses, obtains knowledge of the world around him. In mind over matter (or psychokinesis, as the parapsychologist calls it), the person somehow influences the world around him, without any known forces acting on the object or objects influenced.

Evidently mind over matter does not occur as often as ESP. There have been, however, some rather interesting cases.

Several years ago a family in Long Island was plagued by mysterious happenings in their home. The strange phenomena included ash trays flying across rooms; bottle caps mysteriously screwing off

Mind Over Matter

the bottles, glasses exploding, etc. When parasychologists arrived on the scene to investigate, they could find no ordinary explanation. Physicists and engineers suggested that perhaps vibrations or winds were responsible. These hypotheses couldn't explain everything that happened in the house. What appears to be the correct explanation is that someone in the house was responsible for the events, but that it was his (or her) psychokinetic (mind-over-matter) abilities which were causing the chaos. It is important to notice that this psychokinetic activity was all on an unconscious level. Thus, he might be sitting in his living room and talking with his family, while the unconscious portion of his mind was causing an ashtray to fly across the room and break against a wall 20 feet away!

A more recent case of spontaneous psychokinesis occurred last year in Miami. A company that sold souvenirs of Miami found that their novelties were breaking in the warehouse. Mugs would fall—with apparently no cause—and shatter on the floor. It was found that the breakage occurred only when one particular shipping clerk was present. When all present were watching him, objects from the other side of the warehouse would fly from their shelves and break. Once again the explanation seems to be man's amazing psychokinetic power. Somehow the clerk's mind-over-matter ability was causing all the damage.

As is true of ESP, psychokinetic ability (PK, for short) is mercurial. In such cases the events suddenly, with no apparent reason, cease to occur.

Parapsychologists believe that everyone has the ability to move objects with his mind—even though most of us have not had the problem of paintings flying off our walls or vases mysteriously breaking. Less spectacular events which may be caused by mind over matter often go unrecognized as examples of PK. You may be playing a game with friends and almost all evening the dice will come up to the benefit of one player. If he needs a 3 when he throws the dice a 3 is likely to appear, and so on through the evening. There are similar reports which come out of gambling casinos.

If you would like to see just how much PK you can exert on a pair of dice, you'll find that it's not very difficult to test yourself—and your friends.

The most essential equipment is, of course, a pair of dice. The kind sold in dime stores are quite adequate, as are the kind which come with various games. Basically, what one does is "wish" for a certain result when the pair of dice is thrown. For example, begin by wishing for 1's to appear. Concentrate, and then throw the dice, hoping that 1's will appear. Record the numbers which are uppermost on the dice and then repeat. This is the basic procedure.

Some refinements, however, are necessary. First, it is not advisable to throw the dice by hand. Unconsciously, you may position the dice in your hand at the time of release in such a way as to influence the result. For this reason it is best to use a dice cup, which can be made as follows. Take a 12-ounce beverage can and remove the entire top. This type of can is just the right size so that the

Mind Over Matter

dice, when shaken, will rattle around considerably and be randomized. As an additional precaution you may want to cut up inch-square pieces of corrugated cardboard or similar material and glue 5 of these to the inside of the can at different places along the interior. When the dice are shaken in the cup prior to throwing they will knock against these pieces and be further randomized.

Now that you have your dice and dice cup, only one more requirement need be met for testing. When the dice are thrown, they should be thrown against a backstop of some sort. Almost anything will do. This is to insure additional randomization of the dice after they come out of the cup. A cardboard box set up on a table makes a fine throwing surface. Merely cut out two sides (top and front) and throw into the carton, being certain that the dice always hit the back of the carton. The sides of the carton will stop the dice from rebounding off the table. Now you are fully ready to begin testing.

It is important that you select systematically the numbers you will wish for. That is, you should wish for 1's to come up the same number of times that you wish for 2's, 5's, 4's, 3's, and 6's. The reason follows: If you examine an inexpensive pair of dice you will notice that the numbers are indicated by dots painted in indentations. For the 6-face, 6 indentations are needed; for the 1-face only 1 is necessary. Because of this, the 6-face is lighter (more material was scooped out) than the 1-face. For this reason, the 1-face is heavier and tends to wind up more often on the bottom, and the 6-face, the side opposite, more often on top. This tendency is not very great, but over the long haul it adds up to a considerable effect. If you decided to do all your testing wishing for 6's to appear, you might do very well—not because of mind over matter, but because of that bias. For this reason, all testing should be done wishing for an equal number of appearances of each face. When this is the case, if the bias tendency does show up, you will do well on 6's and poorly on 1's, the results will correct themselves, and your test will be as if you were working with a perfect pair of dice.

A good procedure is to wish for 1's first, then 2's, 3's, 4's, 5's and 6's, in that order. This easy progression will allow you to concentrate. A good number of throws to make in one session is 36. Thus, you can throw 6 times for 1's, 6 times for 2's, etc. This is a long enough run so that you can get a fair idea of how well you are doing and yet not spend so long at it as to become bored.

Every time you make a toss, record how the dice came up. You may want to set up a recording sheet as printed on the next page (Figure 5).

This record sheet shows that John Doe had a total of 20 hits. By chance one expects only 1/6 of all the dice to be hits. (In this case 1/6 of 72 dice is 12.) So Mr. Doe did fairly well.

To see how successful your testing has been, refer to Table 9, on page 98.

Name **John Doe**   Date **1/30**

Session No. **3**   Time **9:05 P.M.**

Target	1	2	3	4	5	6
	5 2	② 6	6 6	5 ④	4 3	⑥ 5
	6 ①	3 4	5 4	6 ④	3 3	5 5
	① 3	② ②	5 6	1 1	② ⑤	4 5
	5 4	1 5	③ 1	2 ④	⑤ 1	⑥ 3
	3 3	3 5	2 1	④ 3	⑤ 4	2 ⑥
	① 5	4 1	③ 4	5 ④	⑤ 3	5 2

| Total | 3 | 3 | 2 | 5 | 4 | 3 |

Figure 5. PK Record Sheet

TABLE 9. Success in Dice Throwing

No. of Runs of 6 tosses (using 2 dice)	Chance	Good (odds of 20 to 1)	Excellent (odds of 100 to 1)
6	12	17	18
12	24	30	32
24	48	57	59
36	72	83	86

As in ESP tests, some light competition in psychokinesis tests often helps results. If you have an interested friend, you might want to alternate throwing the dice. Let your friend toss once for 1's and then you toss for 1's. Repeat this 5 more times, each time recording the actual dice throw. Then go on to 2's, etc. At the end, the player with the highest total wins.

This simple procedure for testing mind over matter is one which can be changed to offer a variety of novel situations. You may want to use different colored dice, to see if you score better when the dice are green rather than red. Or, you might find it interesting to test with different sizes of dice, to see which give the best results. Such changes in procedure may help to keep interest (and scores) high.

CHAPTER X

How to Investigate a "Haunted House"

At the beginning of the previous chapter we briefly mentioned two cases which might easily be classified as "hauntings." In these cases, as in many others, strange physical occurrences took place, apparently with no "normal" explanation. Both of the cases can be called, more properly, *poltergeist* (German for "noisy spirit") cases. In such instances the strange occurrences seem to center around one person. When that person is absent, the occurrences do not take place. The difference between a poltergeist case and a haunting is that in the case of a haunting the inexplicable happenings center around a given location (usually a house, but frequently a church, cemetery, etc.) rather than around a person. The phenomena range widely from lanterns appearing in the dark to doors opening and closing on a windless day.

Reports of hauntings and poltergeists are perhaps more common than one might expect. The

Institute for Parapsychology receives hundreds of letters each year from people who report inexplicable happenings. Frequently they are bothered by these occurrences: children are frightened by noises in the night; parents are concerned that someone will be hurt by flying objects, etc. These letters inevitably ask "what should we do? What causes these strange events?"

Because these reports are so frequent, it is not unlikely that you may have heard of such a haunted house in your neighborhood, or perhaps you have experienced such things yourself. Investigating such cases can often be fun. In this section, we shall try to outline some simple procedures which you can follow when carrying out an investigation of such happenings. Before suggesting that you investigate a haunted house, though, let us assure you that we know of no case where anyone has been injured seriously by these flying objects or related phenomena.

Is There Anything There?

The first thing to do is to find out whether or not there is anything of real interest to investigate. There are many possibilities which will have to be eliminated before you can have any certainty that something paranormal is going on. Of those cases which have been carefully investigated, few turn out to be of interest to the parapsychologist. Frequently a teenage prankster is found to be responsible, or perhaps a squirrel in the attic is behind the noises in the night. The procedures you should follow to eliminate such possibilities will depend on the kind of events reported. Let's discuss these.

Objects moving

If the case you are investigating occurs in someone else's house you will want to observe the objects moving for yourself. By asking when the occurences are most frequent and who is usually present you can determine when it would be best for you to be there. At these times try to have all present behave normally. If you are fortunate enough to see something unusual, then you must begin to determine the cause. If a lamp falls off a table, you must, of course, check to find out whether or not anyone was near enough to pull on an attached cord; if something happens in another room, you must check on whether or not anyone was, or could have been, in the room.

Aside from pranks, trickery can be unconscious. In several cases investigators have discovered that the phenomena were caused by a member of the family who was unaware that he was pulling lamps off the table, throwing small objects, etc., and the entire family was fooled. Such behavior can arise for a variety of psychological reasons, and is not actually pertinent here. Should you discover this to be the case, tact and understanding are essential. Should such be the situation, the investigator should explain the situation to the family and leave the rest for professional help.

If, however, it looks as if there is something of parapsychological interest, then there are several things to do. If small objects have been moving, you might want to place a few target objects around. A small glass bottle placed on a shelf where it is observable by all might be ideal. It might also prove interesting to place some smaller objects under a glass cover (the kind used to cover cakes is fine) to see if they move. Both of these are attempts to gain additional assurance that trickery is not involved. Remember that a magician fools his audience primarily because he determines the course of action. If you control the situation, it will be much less likely that you will be fooled. These are only examples of what can be done, but if you are careful, variations made according to the kinds of phenomena can prove useful.

It should be noted that things rarely happen when there are observers sitting and waiting for them to happen. Rather, something is most likely to occur when your back is turned, just after you've left the room, etc. For this reason it is often best to have two observers so that they can divide their attention.

Noises Heard

Because there is nothing tangible to observe, reports of strange noises, often in the night, are perhaps the most difficult to investigate. The first step in this kind of investigation is to gather reports and see what could normally cause the noises. Then pinpoint the location as well as possible. Should the noises occur while you are present, the best procedure is to attempt to communicate with the source of the noises. (Keep in mind that parapsychologists generally believe the source of such noises to be the unconscious of someone present; somehow that person is unconsciously using his PK ability to cause noises.) One method of communicating is to try to direct express suggestions where you wish the noises to be heard. If the noises have sounded as if they were upstairs, when all are assembled, you might say aloud, "I wish you would knock downstairs where we are." Another way of communicating is by requesting repetitions of the noises. You might use a simple code, such as, "One knock if male, two if female." In this manner you might actually be communicating with someone's unconscious.

Visual Appearances

Another frequently encountered phenomenon is that of unexplained visual images. The ones most frequently reported outside of houses involve lights appearing in the night. In North Carolina, for instance, lights often appear mysteriously on Brown Mountain. Similarly, there are many reports of lights on railroad tracks. Frequently these reports are accompanied by stories of a train disaster, a "ghost" conductor walking the tracks, etc. In spite of the "ghost" conductors, phantom trains, and so on, most of these lights can readily be explained by natural means: reflections on clouds of city lights, optical illusions which make distant lights appear near and a variety of similar explanations. In general, when, during an investigation, one tries to approach these lights, they disappear. This suggests that the effect is an optical one; when the vantage point is changed, the light can't be seen.

Visual phenomena which appear in homes are exceedingly difficult to investigate. Aside from physical causes, hallucination is probably the most frequent explanation of these reports. The Institute for Parapsychology frequently receives reports from people who have "seen ghosts." Sometimes these reports also claim that the apparition told of events in the future which did materialize. This aspect— an accurate prediction of the future—is what

How to Investigate a "Haunted House" 105

makes such a case of parapsychological interest. It involves not merely the seeing of a "ghost" but the gaining of extrasensory information. Since ESP is an unconscious process (one rarely knows how to control it, or even if it is working), a possible explanation for such cases involving knowledge of the future obtained from "ghosts" is as follows: We know that everyone, to some extent, has ESP. Thus, a person who had a vision of this nature may have used *his* ESP (precognition) to obtain knowledge of the future. This knowledge was on an unconscious level, and the mode by which it emerged was through hallucination. Often people will doubt their own ESP ability, but believe that "ghosts" have such powers. Thus, in order to bring their knowledge gained by ESP to consciousness, they conjure up ghosts. When apparition cases are investigated, rarely do the investigators see anything of interest.

Should you become involved in such a strange set of circumstances, there is one avenue of approach which might be both fruitful and exciting. If you do learn of a recurring and predicting "ghost," then why not ask it questions—or ask the person who sees it to ask questions. You might start with a prediction of which playing card you will randomly select from a deck of 52. If, by some chance, this works, then you can proceed to ask it when it will leave the household!

A Different Approach

There is a rather interesting and different approach to investigating "ghosts" which was developed by Dr. Gertrude Schmeidler of City College, New York. You and your friends may find this approach fun to try.

A friend told Dr. Schmeidler that she—the friend—thought her house was haunted. What was of extreme interest was that the three other members of the family agreed on where the ghost had appeared and also on what kind of personality he had. This agreement seemed to indicate that there might really be something there, and led Dr. Schmeidler to creating a new approach to the investigation of such phenomena.

She obtained a floor plan of the house and divided it into equal areas. She then asked the members of the family to tell her which areas were most often frequented by the ghost. She also asked them to check the items on a list of adjectives which they felt applied to the ghost. Thus, if they felt he was friendly, a check would be placed next to that adjective. Below is the list Dr. Schmeidler used.

Adjective Checklist for the Ghost

active	contented	greedy	noisy
affectionate	cruel	headstrong	obliging
aggressive	demanding	helpful	patient

How to Investigate a "Haunted House"

alert	despondent	humorous	peaceable
aloof	determined	immature	quiet
anxious	dignified	impatient	rigid
apathetic	distrustful	impulsive	shy
arrogant	emotional	independent	stern
bitter	enterprising	irritable	strong
calm	fearful	jolly	submissive
changeable	forceful	leisurely	tolerant
cold	forgiving	mature	trusting
complaining	friendly	meek	vindictive
confused	gentle	mischievous	warm
			weak

Now she had an indication of what the people felt the ghost was like, and where its haunts were. She then, in the absence of the family, had people who felt they were sensitive to such matters taken on a tour of the house. These people next indicated on copies of the floor plan the areas where *they* felt the ghost had appeared. They also had copies of the adjective checklist, and checked the characteristics that they felt applied to the uninvited guest.

The idea, of course, was to see if the entirely separate impressions of the sensitives were in agreement with what the family reported. When Dr. Schmeidler compared the lists, there were some striking correspondences. She used a relatively complicated statistical evaluation, but if you would like to try a version of this technique, a simpler procedure may be adequate for our purposes here.

You might want to try the method with friends who feel they are especially sensitive. After they have been over the house, checked the floor plan and adjectives, you will want to see if their reports correspond to the reports of those who have seen the ghost. A simplified way of doing this is to note into how many areas you have divided your floor plan. If you have 10 areas, say, and the ghost has appeared in only one, then the chances are 10 to 1 against someone picking that area as the one in which the ghost appears. In the case of the checklist, there are 57 adjectives. Let's say that those who report the case check 10 adjectives as describing the ghost. Then, for any adjective checked by someone else, the odds are about 5½ to one (10 in 57) that it will be one of the 10 checked by those reporting the case.

The above are only rules of thumb which may help you to decide if there is a correspondence between what is reported by those who see the ghost and what your friends' impressions are.

As you can see, we have not given odds against chance in discussing the results of such a procedure. One problem involved in such a procedure is that even a striking correspondence between reports may only indicate that all the people involved have similar ideas of what a ghost should be like and what kinds of places it should frequent. Consequently, good results may not indicate that all the participants have sensed the same thing.

Although this method of investigation is not as objective as others we have discussed, it is one which can be fun and perhaps indicative of an unusual phenomenon.

Ghost Hunting Rules

We have given some specific suggestions as to how one might investigate a haunted house. Because they are so specific, they may be of little practical value should you have the opportunity of investigating a poltergeist case. Here are some general rules on "ghost hunting" that may come in handy.

It is best to avoid publicity. Newspapers are often eager for such stories, as they make interesting reading. The presence of newspapermen and others who flock to the scene can only hinder your investigation. Similarly, people who are suggestible, easily excited, etc., also hinder objective investigations. On the other hand, local professional people may be helpful in conducting your investigation. Doctors, ministers, lawyers and other professional people have proven helpful in several instances in the past.

In your investigation, detailed records will help considerably in the overall evaluation of a case. (If possible, have a fellow investigator keep an independent record so that you can check each other for accuracy.) Photographs and tape recordings may prove quite useful, if these can be quickly and efficiently assembled. If you are fortunate enough to come across a poltergeist case, you will probably find investigating it a challenge. Inevitably there will be obstacles which you will have to overcome. Should you succeed in successfully and objectively investigating a legitimate poltergeist case, we believe you will find it quite rewarding and eagerly await your next case. Perhaps now is the time to rouse that ghost in the attic.

CHAPTER XI

What Next?

By now you are somewhat expert on how to test for ESP (and even mind over matter). But there is a lot more to ESP testing than we have been able to show you in these chapters. The purpose of this section will be to give you some tips for advanced work, and also to let you know where you can get the additional information you might want.

In any ESP testing, one is looking for evidence of ESP. So far we have looked at the two most obvious indicators of ESP: above-chance scoring and below-chance scoring. There are many other indicators of ESP, but we could not possibly discuss all of them in this limited space. Rather, let us give you one clue to look for. When you see this clue, you can be sure ESP is at work in one of its manifestations. Be on the lookout for *strange* fluctuations in the individual scores on the ESP tests you give. To make this point clear, let me give an exaggerated example.

Imagine that you are giving someone the Four Aces Test, and he decides to try it 6 times. We know that by chance he is expected to get 12 hits when he matches 48 cards against the aces. Let's say that the person you test gets the following scores on his 6 tries at the test: 0, 24, 0, 24, 0, 24. It is obvious that something interesting is going on. He has scored considerably below chance on three of these tests and considerably above chance on the other three tests. The odds against a score of either 0 or 24 are greater than 100 to 1, so it is clear that ESP is the cause of this strange set of scores. It appears as though, for some reason, the person tested has alternated positive and negative ESP. It is important to note that if we were merely to add up his scores on all 6 runs, the total would be 72, which is exactly the total to be expected by chance (12 x 6). Thus, if this were our only indicator of ESP, we would not have seen that ESP was indeed operating. The moral of the story is, keep your eyes open for fluctuating scores.

You may be asking, "How much do scores have to fluctuate to indicate that ESP is operating?" This is a good question, but one to which there is no easy or general answer. The statistics involved in figuring out the significance of fluctuations are relatively complicated, so you will have to rely on your subjective impressions as to whether or not there is considerable fluctuation. With experience in testing, and examination of scores, you will eventually gain an idea of how much fluctuation is unusual. If you are not satisfied with this subjective evaluation, and wish to know the odds against whatever fluctuations

What Next?

show up in the scores you obtain, we will tell you how to calculate this later in this section.

We have seen above that a large amount of fluctuation in scores is an indicator of ESP. When we considered high scoring as an indicator, we found there was a surprising counterpart—low scoring. The same is true of high fluctuations; that is you should also be on the lookout for low fluctuations. Perhaps one last example will help you see this more clearly.

In the testing you have done by now, you have probably gotten at least one series in which the scores average out to pretty close to what one would expect by chance. Let us say that in this series you used the Four Aces Test and the average score you obtained was very close to chance—12. You will have noticed, however, that not all your scores were 12's. Your average of 12 was obtained by adding some scores of 12, but also some scores of 10, 11, 13, 14, etc. One doesn't expect only 12's; some fluctuation or deviation is expected. Thus, you should also be surprised if you do a series of tests and every score is exactly at chance. This lack of fluctuation is also an indicator of ESP! Just what causes people to score consistently exactly at chance, and how their ESP works to accomplish this strange task, is not yet completely understood. Parapsychologists are working on this question right now, and perhaps this mystery will soon be solved.

To review very briefly, you now have the four major indicators of ESP for which you can look in your tests: high scoring and low scoring; and high fluctuations and low fluctuations. There are more indicators, but if you are on the lookout for these four you should be able to spot ESP, wherever it may be lurking.

Your repertoire of ESP tests is by now relatively large. Even so, after you have tried them all and have acquired a feeling for ESP testing you will undoubtedly be looking for new tests and variations you can try. Here you are limited only by your imagination. One general variation which often is interesting to those tested is changing the objects that are being guessed. If, for example, you have been using playing cards in your testing, you may want to switch to something more appropriate to the person you are testing. If he is an artist, you might take a set of 20 index cards and write the name of one color on 5 of the cards, another color on another 5, etc. Thus, he could guess colors, which might interest him and inspire high scoring. When making a deck of testing cards out of index cards you must be very careful. Hold an index card up to the light and you will find how easy it is to see through. For this reason, if you are using such a deck of cards, it is best to shuffle the deck out of sight of the person being tested and then place it in a box, or cover the deck with something opaque. This will insure that your results will be due to ESP and not to unconscious peeking.

Another change which might be enjoyable for all is the use of a standard ESP deck. There is nothing magical about the cards themselves, but the use of a professional deck may add considerably to the atmosphere of the experiment. You can purchase an ESP deck from:

The Institute for Parapsychology
Box 6847, College Station
Durham, North Carolina 27708

The price is $1.00 and this includes a supply of ESP Record Sheets and a set of instructions.

Another dollar item which is available at the above address and which you might find helpful is *Manual for Introductory Experiments in Parapsychology* by Dr. Louisa E. Rhine. One part of the manual which you may find especially useful deals with experimental projects which you can try. In this section, Dr. Rhine discusses some more advanced projects not covered in this book.

In thinking about ESP and some of the tests covered in this book you may well come up with some experiments and ideas of your own you want to test. Sometimes you will be able to design an experiment which will test your idea; sometimes you will not. If you run into a problem which you cannot solve, the research staff of the Institute for Parapsychology will be glad to help in any way they can. Just write to them and state your problem or question as simply as possible. Another area in which the Institute can help is in evaluating the results of your testing. In this book we have given guidelines which should help in evaluating your test results. However, because we wish to keep the procedure of basic ESP testing as clear as possible, we have not given instructions which would enable you to evaluate *all* the possible results you may obtain. If in your testing you obtain results which you feel may be of interest, but on which you do not know how to figure the odds, again, the research staff of the Institute for Parapsychology will be glad to help.

We know that *you* are interested in parapsychology, or else you wouldn't be reading this book. However, you probably have friends who are also interested in the subject. Should they be sufficiently interested to want to do some testing, it might be a good idea to form a parapsychology club, with weekly or monthly meetings. There are many advantages to forming such a club. When deciding on an experiment to conduct, you will have the benefit of discussion with the other members. Once the experiment is underway, you can help each other with the problems which may arise, and can even use each other as subjects in the experiments. Many clubs which started in such a small way have made important contributions to parapsychology through their experiments. Also, once your club is established, you may find various civic clubs requesting speakers on ESP. Giving talks to local groups can be quite rewarding and enjoyable, and is just one of the possible benefits of forming a parapsychology club.

As you can see, in this section we are making suggestions in areas which are beyond the scope just of ESP testing. Perhaps the most important thing we can do is to suggest additional reading material which may answer your questions not covered in this book. Below, on page 137, several books are described which we feel are suitable for the layman. We hope we have interested you enough to try some of them.

AFTERWORD

Can You Communicate Drawings?

by Andrea Fodor Litkei[*]

You are sitting in a room on the north side of the house, while your little daughter is in her playroom, on the south side. You have agreed that you will draw a simple black-and-white picture at 3:00 in the afternoon. The clock strikes 3:00. You draw, to the best of your ability, a fierce lion, complete with mane and tail. A few moments later, your daughter comes scooting into your room: she has drawn, clumsily but quite clearly, a pussycat.

What have we here? Telepathy? Clairvoyance? Or nothing at all?

In the simplest terms, you have done an ESP experiment with drawings. It doesn't really matter

---

[*] Andrea Fodor Litkei is the author of *ESP: An Account of the Fabulous in Our Everyday Life* and of a volume of poetry, *Thalassa*. Mrs. Litkei is the daughter of the late Dr. Nandor Fodor, noted psychoanalyst and psychical researcher. Her writings have appeared in several anthologies, notably *The Psychic Reader* (New York, 1969); she contributed the paper "Precognition—Or Telepathy from the Past?" to *The Psychoanalytic Review*, Vol. 56, No. 1, 1969.

117

whether telepathy or clairvoyance was at work—whether your daughter was "reading your mind" or somehow "seeing" the drawing of the lion independently; ESP *was* probably at work. Tests such as this, only more carefully controlled and evaluated, are among the easiest, most entertaining and potentially useful experiments in extrasensory perception. Similar experiments, undertaken under laboratory conditions, today offer a fruitful field of research. But even outside the laboratory, drawing tests can be performed by almost anyone so inclined. Naturally, the experience of others can caution you against fooling yourself, against going overboard at the first flush of enthusiasm, should you achieve success. But, by using proper methods —particularly in evaluation of the results—you may not only discover unsuspected talents within yourself, but, by adhering to the rules of the game, you may come up with a series of tests that could prove scientifically valuable.

Basically, the methods are simple; but, as we have said, the evaluation of the final drawings is not. Let's first of all concentrate on just how to go about setting up a drawing test. It is not something you can force yourself to do; no amount of "willing" the drawings into the minds of another is likely to guarantee success. As in other ESP experiments and in many other phenomena of nature, human or otherwise, good results often appear quite independently of man's will.

To begin at the beginning:

You have two people. One is the agent who does the "sending." The other, the percipient, does the

Can You Communicate Drawings? 119

"receiving." As in the mother-and-child test, the simplest of these experiments is for the agent to make a drawing—separated from the percipient, of course—while the percipient tries to "pick-up" this drawing in some form or other whether through the agent's mind (telepathy) or by perceiving the drawing independently (clairvoyance). The percipient should draw something that is a reasonable facsimile of the picture the agent puts on paper, without benefit of normal channels of communication, hints, clues or anything else that would give the game away.

All this sounds easy enough. But some preparation of both agent and percipient is necessary. It goes without saying that the two should be well separated. Even among the most conscientious and honest experimenters, unconscious clues are sometimes given. Let some experienced and uninvolved observers sit in on the experiment, preferably at both ends. Some psychologists believe that an ESP-perceived image undergoes an unconscious change in the percipient's mind (perhaps in the agent's as well). This means that an idea or image, as it is transmitted, is somehow distorted—it may reflect some unconscious absorption, elements of daydreaming, some barely observed outside distraction or just any old fragment of thought or impression that happens to get tangled up with the "transmission," as on a telephone party line.

A series of fascinating experiments in drawings were undertaken by the writer Upton Sinclair, best known for his book, *The Jungle*. Together with his wife, Mary, Sinclair conducted a series of drawing experiments, which he published in a book entitled *Mental Radio* (New York, 1930). Mary Sinclair, who was the percipient in these experiments, put down some observations that may come in handy. They do not apply to everyone, but they are useful guidelines for percipients; she wrote:

"Relax the body as completely as possible . . . visualize a rose, or a violet—some pleasant, familiar thing which does not arouse emotional memory trains . . . Keep attention steady, just seeing the color, or shape of the flower and nothing else. Do not think things about the flower. Just look at it." For practice, before trying with the agent, she continues, "Ask someone to draw a half-dozen simple designs for you on cards, or on slips of paper, and to fold them so that you cannot see the contents. They should be folded separately, so that you can handle them one at a time. . . . My experience is that fragments of forms appear first. For example, a curved line, or a straight one, or two lines of a triangle. But sometimes they are so vague that one gets only a notion of how they look before they vanish."

Before discussing the agent's role, the type of drawings that seem best suited for this type of experiment and other details, let me give an example of a direct hit from Sinclair experiments. It not only illustrates an encouraging and positive result, but also the way in which the unconscious may latch on to the symbolic content of an image to such a degree that the image itself is in danger of being swamped completely out of the transmission.

Mary Sinclair and Robert Irwin, the husband of

Can You Communicate Drawings? 121

her younger sister, made an arrangement that at a certain hour each day, Bob, in his home in Pasadena, was to take pencil and paper, make a drawing of an object and sit and concentrate in his mind on that drawing. At the same hour, Mary Sinclair, in her home in Long Beach, 40 miles away, was to give orders to her unconscious mind to find out what was in Bob's mind. The drawings were to be dated and filed, and when the two of them met they would compare the results in the presence of Upton Sinclair and Bob's wife. Bob's first drawing was done on a half sheet of green paper. The word "CHAIR" underneath, and the date, were written by Bob, while the words "drawn by Bob Irwin" were added for the purpose of record by Mary Sinclair (Figures 6 and 6a)

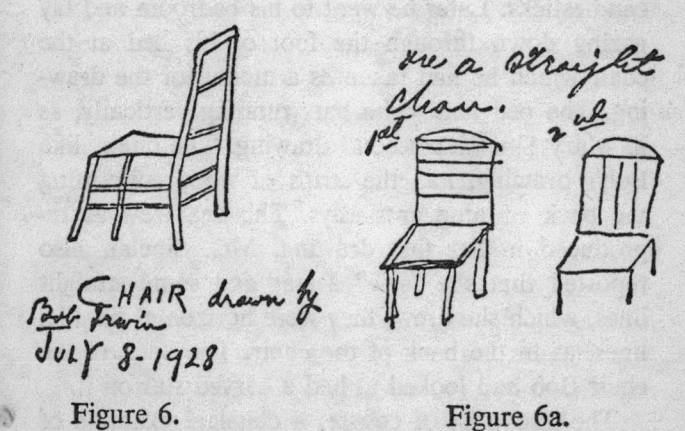

Figure 6.   Figure 6a.

According to Mary Sinclair, at 10:00 a.m. or a little before on this day, she was sewing and "saw" Bob taking something from a black sideboard; she thought it was a glass candlestick. At 11:15, now concentrating, she saw Bob sitting at a dining room table—a dish or some small object in front of him (on the northeast corner of the table). She tried to see what it was—a white something. She couldn't decide and concentrated on seeing his drawing on a green paper. It was now about 11:20, and she thought that he had made his drawing. She tried to see the paper with the drawing on it and saw a straight chair. She wasn't sure of her second drawing because it *did not seem to be on his paper*. She thought it might be his bedfoot. She distinctly saw a chair like the first on his paper, Figure 6a.

Later, when the above test was under discussion, Mary Sinclair learned that Bob had sat at the northeast corner of the table, trying to decide what to draw, and facing the sideboard on which were silver candlesticks. Later he went to his bedroom and lay gazing down through the foot of his bed at the chair which he had taken as a model for the drawing. The bed had white bars running vertically, as in Mary Sinclair's second drawing. The chair, like Bob's drawing, had the strips of wood supporting the back running crossways. This feature was reproduced in her first drawing. Mrs. Sinclair also reported that she "saw" a star and some straight lines, which she drew; they were horizontal parallel lines, as in the back of the chair. The back of the chair Bob had looked at had a carved star on it.

The above is, of course, a classical example of ESP in a gifted psychic, but it does serve to show the meanderings of even these perceptions. Mary Sinclair could just as well have drawn a candlestick, been totally off the mark and yet have attained evidence for a telepathic perception. However, one should not go off in the other direction and read all sorts of meanings into two drawings that have no apparent relationship, and be spurred on by nothing more than the will to believe.

Little is known as to who is more important in such tests, the agent or the percipient. It is necessary for the percipient to be sensitive to the message at the moment of experiment, therefore it may not be enough for the message to be "well sent."

It has been suggested that emotion tone may have an effect on telepathic transmission. The emotional content becomes important because the emergence of a telepathic image is a collaboration of the conscious mind with the unconscious, via symbols often loaded with emotional content—which are only later interpreted by the intellect. In fact it is possible that an agent may ruin his sending by inadvertently having other thoughts of stronger emotional content at the time of his drawing. This is why it might be best for the agent to be in a relaxed state of mind.

Coincidence is another annoying factor, which can only be eliminated through long, arduous experimentation analyzed by minute, detailed statistics. However, if you should be fortunate enough to run into a lot of striking "coincidences," and always with the same people conducting the particular experiment, then you are fairly safe in thinking you may have something more than coincidence.

The type of sketch or image that the agent is trying to send to the percipient should contain some elements of emotion but not tragic elements since the unconscious of the percipient may reject them in self-defense. Also, keep the drawings as simple as possible, especially at the beginning.

For practice, it might be a good idea to follow the example of an actual training experiment, from the French magazine *Revue Métapsychique* (March, 1966), "Recherche d'une Méthode d'entrainement à la Télépathie (Research of a method for training in telepathy), by Henri Marcotte:

1. The percipient imagines an arbitrary drawing (A) which is not the drawing of the agent (B). Agent and percipient are, of course, separated. The percipient then notes a following transformation of image A independently of his conscious will. According to Marcotte, image A will tend to transform itself into image B.

2. The agent takes three simple abstract figures (triangle, square, cross, circle, etc.) and concentrates on one of them. The percipient should try to visualize each of the three figures and take note of how they appear without making up his mind as to which one of the three is being sent by the agent. Hopefully one of them will then appear more luminous and its contours will be more easily discerned than other two.

3. A flash method: The percipient should imagine a complete blackness in front of him and at a signal from the agent (ringing a bell, for example) imagine that a bright light is flood-

ing the paper in front of the agent on which he is doing his drawing.

Now we come to the problem: Is it best for percipient and agent to know each other well? In the scientific experimental situation, when the agent and the percipient share a common set of experiences, the telepathic process may be influenced adversely. The chain of common associations tends to confuse the outcome, making correct evaluation extremely difficult. Both agent and percipient can be misled, by their common associations, into believing in the telepathic situation, whereas the coincidences may be due to a common trend of thought. On the other hand, either may unconsciously avoid a suggestion because he knows it exists in the other person. The very opposite seems to be true, though, when telepathy occurs spontaneously in life situations. However, the work of C. E. Stuart, who has reported several studies in the paranormal perception of drawings, showed that under experimental conditions, "closely related pairs (twins, married couples and engaged couples) gave significantly positive results," in contrast with the scores of unrelated pairs.

Having tried these experiments within your family, which is the easiest and most convenient way to start, you may want to wander further afield and try it with friends and lesser known acquaintances; you may want to experiment with five or more people—with one agent sending—and keep scores as to who is the best recipient. This can be done by mail, with letters timed so that they cross each other, by telephone or by prearranged group gatherings. (The presence of witnesses will make your experiment more scientific.) If you do a series, then be sure that the drawings are filed and numbered correctly. The percipients must never, of course, know what is being drawn, by either clues or inadvertent suggestions from the agents. Keep records of *all* runs, the errors as well as the hits. Certain associations may dawn on you at a later date, enabling you to evaluate them more correctly.

You might want to try Upton and Mary Sinclair's method. He would make drawings on slips of paper and put them in envelopes. Mary Sinclair, while lying down, would put one of the envelopes on her solar plexus, believing it might be the center of unknown forces. Sinclair would watch her until she felt she had the right answer and then they would compare the results. The curious thing was that sometimes the second drawing was registered in her mind before she finished the first one. For example, she felt a necktie had been drawn but she added puffs of smoke at the end of her tie. The *next* drawing that Sinclair handed to her in the sealed envelope was, in this instance, of a burning match. You will probably have noticed that this sounds more like a clairvoyance experiment (receiving the drawings, rather than Upton Sinclair's thoughts) than a telepathy experiment. It is very difficult to devise a "pure telepathy" experiment. Thus, when we talk of telepathy, clairvoyance could also be the explanation for good results.

Can You Communicate Drawings?

There is a classical example of an experiment *a quatre*, done in the early nineteen hundreds, carried out at Liverpool, by a Mr. Malcolm Guthrie, J.P., head of a local firm, and a Mr. James Birchall, the honorary secretary of the Liverpool Literary and Philosophical Society. Mr. Guthrie and Mr. Birchall were the agents and a Miss Edwards and a Miss Relph, two young ladies in the employ of Mr. Guthrie's firm, were the percipients. In the following four selected samples of the series there was no physical contact between agents and percipients.

Note that with the exception of one, the circle with the cross on top (Fig. 8), none of the drawings are identical, but the thoughts behind them have been transmitted and reproduced within the modifications of the recipients' own minds. These happen to be beautifully clear examples; there are many which are not, and yet, on correct analysis, may still hold up under analysis as the result of telepathy.

This brings us to the problem of training oneself for intellectual acrobatics and yet at the same time being wary of going overboard. G. N. M. Tyrrell, the well-known psychic researcher, has said:

"The conscious experience of the percipient, whether it takes the form of a vision or a voice or a dream or an impulse, is a *created symbol* which stands for the telepathic event. It is not the telepathic event itself, but is a signal created to inform

Figure 7.

ORIGINAL DRAWING   **REPRODUCTION**

Mr. Birchall and Miss Relph. No contact.

ORIGINAL DRAWING

Mr. Birchall and Miss Relph. No contact.

REPRODUCTION

Miss Relph said she seemed to see a lot of rings, as if they were moving, and she could not get them steadily before her eyes.

Figure 8.

ORIGINAL DRAWING   **REPRODUCTION**

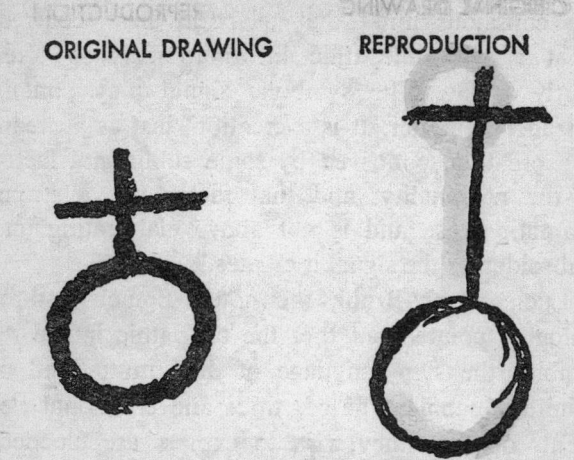

Mr. Guthrie and Miss Edwards. No contact.

ORIGINAL DRAWING

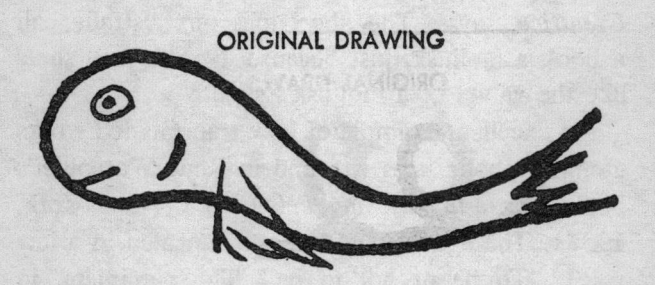

Mr. Guthrie and Miss Edwards. No contact.

REPRODUCTION

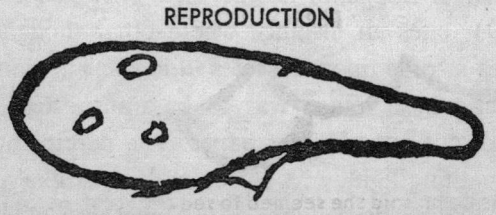

Miss Edwards almost directly said, "Are you thinking of the bottom of the sea, with shells and fishes?" and then, "Is it a snail or a fish?" — then drew as above.

the conscious mind that telepathy has occurred. That is why telepathic information is so often partly wrong. The symbolic signal may contain extraneous matter. It is a creation, just as a dream is a creation, contrived by some subliminal factor in the personality; and that factor has a strong dramatic sense and is not above elaborating and embroidering the signal it creates."

Lucien Lévy-Bruhl, the noted French anthropologist, pointed out that the telepathic image resembles the sign language of deaf mutes and of primitive people. The cognitive and emotional elements of what they wish to express are blended. Feelings as well as formal and logical meanings are conveyed. Ribot, in his *Essai Sur L'imagination Creatrice*, says, "The aborigines of Australia call a book a mollusk, just because it opens and shuts like the valves of a mollusk's shell."

An excellent example of how transmission works along symbolic lines is found in René Warcollier's book, *Experiments in Telepathy* (New York, 1938). The agent, in one room, repeated in a low voice, "To be or not to be." The percipient, in another room, thought of a cross in a graveyard! Sir Oliver Lodge, in *The Survival of Man* (London, 1909), cites an instance where other thought processes intrude upon the telepathic transmission. The object whose image was to be transmitted was a teapot cut out of silver paper. The percipient said, "Something light. . . . No color. Looks like a duck . . . like a silver duck. . . . Something oval. . . .

Head at one end and tail at the other." The agent explained that during the experiment he had been thinking how much that teapot resembled a duck.

The agent's and the percipient's minds, when they are attuned, become one during the moment of telepathic transmission, and all causes of error are common to both, resulting in a distorted image that has to be unraveled with care, taking into account the associations, at the time, of both participants.

Further to confuse the evaluations of the drawings for the inexperienced, we have; (1) Fragmentation, (2) Multiplication, (3) Inversion and (4) Condensation—to mention a few.

Regarding fragmentation: In the case of an agent's drawing a geometric figure, let us say a square, the recipient may receive the image of two or more right angles scattered in space, not four straight lines joined together. Concentric circles are often received as nests of detached arcs. In other words, movement has been injected into what would otherwise be a static image. The mind of the recipient is, in this case, only able to express the image through the addition of the dynamic quality of movement, resulting in fragmentation.

Multiplication: Parts of the drawing are repeated several times—just as in dream images—or there is repetition of the same words and gestures.

Inversion: For example, a long fish with its head at the right, may be represented by the recipient as a very fat fish with its head at the left, as was shown in experiments by René Warcollier in 1929.

An interesting example of a percipient ignoring the emotional tone of an agent is an experiment wherein a tactile sensation, on the part of the agent, was transformed into a visual image. Warcollier, as agent, shut himself up in complete darkness in his photographic laboratory. He then wound a cord very tightly around his index finger and left it there for five minutes. He experienced actual pain localized at the end of the finger. He did not think of the percipient but only of the discomfort which he renewed by unwinding and rewinding the cord. He had not only a tactile sensation, but also a quasi-visual image of the bound-up finger, especially of its extremity. After five minutes, when he turned on the light and unbound the finger, he was surprised by the deep ridges on the finger, the end of which was red and misshapen.

Bonnet, his percipient, first perceived a form which he associated with the trunk of a tree, then a branch of a tree, then a gun barrel and finally the exact form of a finger. The exaggeration of the size of the fingertip corresponded much more to Warcollier's sensations than to objective reality; the ridges, as perceived, corresponded, on the contrary, more to the reality than to Warcollier's conscious impression. Finally, Bonnet drew a bundle of faggots and explained this as something in a circle. The idea of the imaginary tree still prevailed, but he received no impression of the sensation of pain.

To all the known factors, and to so many yet

unknown, another factor should be added, and that is the time element. Experience has pointed to the fact that telepathic communication is not always instantaneous. The telepathic image is not necessarily received the moment that it is sent. Spontaneous and experimental situations have shown that sometimes there is a time lag which can last a few seconds, a few minutes, or may extend over a period of several days. If the time lag is long—when a drawing is the telepathic target—a secondary elaboration may take place which frequently gives rise to a large number of associations that attach themselves to the impression that is received. In a paper read before the Vienna Psychoanalytic Society in 1922, Freud has this to say on time and telepathy: ". . . no one has the right to take exception to telepathic occurrences on the ground that the event and the presentiment (or message) do not exactly coincide in astronomical time. It is perfectly conceivable that a telepathic message might arrive contemporaneously with the event and yet only penetrate to consciousness the following night during sleep, or even in waking life after a while, during some pause in the activity of the mind."

What we have examined so far may be all quite fascinating, but it has the disadvantage of avoiding the question of careful evaluation. The reason for this is simple: Few people have the training or patience to apply quantitative and statistical methods to an amusing or even awe-inspiring parlor game, even if it is called "telepathy" or "clairvoyance." And yet, it isn't really all that forbidding to try to make sure that your final results will stand up to fairly rigid scrutiny. If you would like to go beyond the parlor-game stage of ESP drawings, you should study the literature in the field; not only the books and articles I have mentioned, but the more technical articles that have appeared in the *Journal of Parapsychology*. A listing of them can be found at the end of this essay.

Your most important control is the final judging of the results. The crucial question, in the end, always is: Just how closely does the percipient's drawing resemble the agent's original? There is a danger in reading too much resemblance into them. For this reason it is essential, if one is serious about these experiments, to let the final comparison be made by independent judges. For instance, Dr. J. H. Rush and Mrs. Ann Jensen, back in 1949, made 50 trials of reproducing drawings, over distances of from 200 to 500 miles (not much chance of unconscious clues at that distance!). The results were statistically significant, which means that more similarities were found than could be expected by chance. You do not have to use a complicated judging procedure to gain some indication of whether or not ESP is involved. We can give a somewhat simplified method of evaluation which you may wish to try.

It is most important to have someone evaluate the drawings who does not know what is expected. An example will help illustrate this. Let's say that

Can You Communicate Drawings? 135

10 times an agent has drawn a picture which a percipient has tried to reproduce. Thus, after your experiment, you have 20 pictures: 10 targets and 10 attempts at duplication. Now, shuffle the set of 10 target pictures and place them in an envelope marked "targets." Then do the same for the remaining 10 pictures and place them in an envelope marked "reproduction." These two envelopes are then given to a judge who knows nothing about the experiment. He is to lay out the 10 target pictures in front of him. His job, of course, is now to take the 10 "reproductions" and try to match them with their targets. If he thinks a drawing of a fish looks considerably like a drawing of a cigar, then he places these two together. He does this till all 10 "reproductions" are matched. If he wishes, he may place two "reproductions" by one target picture, should he feel that they both strongly resemble that target. In this case, we know that at least one will be mismatched, but this is not crucial since we don't expect 100 per cent success.

The judge should do his matching while alone (to avoid unconscious sensory cues) and should take all the time he feels is needed. After he has made his decisions, the participants in the experiment can see how many times the judge has matched the target with the correct reproduction. By chance, you would expect the judge to have only one correct matching. If he has two, this may be a slight indication that ESP was involved. Three matchings can be considered good, and if there are four or more matchings, then the results are excellent. This method of evaluation is, of course, not exact, but it will serve as a good rule-of-thumb to decide if anything more than coincidence was operating.

References

Drawings as Targets

Pratt, J. G., "The Work of Dr. C. Hilton Rice in Extrasensory Perception." *Journal of Parapsychology*, 1937, *1*, 239–59.

Rush, J. H. and Jensen, Ann., A Reciprocal Distance GESP Test with Drawings. *Journal of Parapsychology*, 1949, *13*, 122–34.

Stuart, C. E., An ESP Experiment with Enclosed Drawings." *Journal of Parapsychology*, 1945, *9*, 278–95.

———, "The Carington Free-Drawing Approach to the ESP Problem." *Journal of Parapsychology*, 1944, *8*, 127–38.

———, "An ESP Test with Drawings." *Journal of Parapsychology*, 1942, *6*, 20–43.

———, "Personality Measurements and ESP Tests with Cards and Drawings." *Journal of Parapsychology*, 1947, *11*, 118–146.

SUGGESTED READINGS

Spontaneous Case Studies

Hidden Channels of the Mind by Louisa E. Rhine. Spontaneous experiences. New York: William Sloane, 1961. $5.00 Also New York: Apollo Editions, 1965. $1.95 (paperback).

ESP in Life and Lab by Louisa E. Rhine. A bridge between experiences and experiments. New York: Macmillan, 1967. $5.95.

General Introductions to Research

Parapsychology Today edited by J. B. Rhine and Robert Brier. First of a series of annual cross-section reviews of current international psi research, edited and arranged for both lay and professional readers. Twenty-three authors report their own researches or appraise the present status of the field. New York: Citadel Press, 1968. $6.00.

The Reach of the Mind by J. B. Rhine. Step-by-step review of original ESP and PK researches. Sketch of experimental advances. New York: Apollo Editions, 1961. $1.95 (paperback).

Test Materials

ESP cards with elementary instructions and 25 record sheets. $1.00 a set. For fuller elementary instructions, see *Manual* (below).

ESP record pads (50 sheets). Fifty cents.

Manual for Introductory Experiments in Parapsychology. Elementary articles and test instructions for both ESP and PK experiments. Suitable for students and others beginning the study of parapsychology. Durham: Parapsychology Press, 1966. $1.00 (multilithed).

The above books and test materials are available from:
 The Institute for Parapsychology
 Box 6847, College Station
 Durham, North Carolina 27708

GLOSSARY

AGENT: The "sender" in tests for telepathy; the person whose mental images are the targets to be apprehended by the percipient. In General ESP (GESP) tests, the person who looks at the target object.

CALL: The subject's guess in trying to identify the target in an ESP test.

CHANCE (*Mean Chance Expectation, Chance Expectation and Chance Average*): The most likely score if only chance is involved.

CLAIRVOYANCE: Extrasensory perception of objects or objective events.

DEVIATION: The amount an observed number of successes varies (either above or below) from mean chance expectation of a run, series or other unit of trials in testing for ESP.

DT (DOWN THROUGH): The clairvoyance testing technique in which the cards are called down through the entire pack before any is removed or checked.

ESP (EXTRASENSORY PERCEPTION): Experience of or response to a target object, state, event or influence without sensory contact.

ESP CARDS: Cards, each bearing one of the following five symbols: star, circle, square, cross and waves (three parallel wavy lines). A standard pack has 25 cards.

    Closed Pack: An ESP pack, composed of five each of the five symbols.

    Open Pack: An ESP pack made up of the ESP symbols selected in random order, thereby being composed of no fixed number of each symbol.

FREE MATERIAL: Target objects in ESP tests in which the range of possible targets is unspecified.

GESP: (GENERAL EXTRASENSORY PERCEPTION): ESP which could be either telepathy or clairvoyance or both.

PARANORMAL (PARAPSYCHICAL, PARAPSYCHOLOGICAL): Attributable to psi. (See PSI.)

PARAPSYCHOLOGY: The branch of science that deals with psi communication, i.e., behavioral or personal exchanges which are extrasensorimotor—not dependent on the senses and muscles.

PERCIPIENT: The person experiencing ESP; also, one who is tested for ESP ability.

PK (PSYCHOKINESIS): The extramotor aspect of psi; a direct (i.e., mental but nonmuscular) influence exerted by the subject on an external physical process, condition or object.

PRECOGNITION: Prediction of future events, i.e., random events, the occurrence of which cannot be inferred from present knowledge.

PSI (PARAPSYCHICAL, PARAPSYCHOLOGICAL): A general term to identify extrasensorimotor exchange with the environment. Psi includes ESP and PK.

PSI DIFFERENTIAL EFFECT: Significant difference between scoring rates when subjects are participating in an experiment which has two comparative conditions (such as two types of targets or two modes of response).

PSI-HITTING, PSI-MISSING: Excerise of psi ability in a way that hits (psi-hitting) or avoids (psi-missing) the target the subject is attempting.

PSI PHENOMENA: Occurrences which result from the operation of psi. (See PSI.)

PSYCHICAL RESEARCH: Original term for parapsychology.

RANDOM ORDER: Chance arrangements.

RUN: In psi tests, a standard group of trials. In ESP tests the run is usually 25 trials based on the deck of 25 ESP cards or symbols; in PK tests the standard run consists of 24 single die throws regardless of the number of dice thrown together.

SCORE: The number of hits made in any given unit of trials, usually a run.

   Total Score: Pooled scores of all runs.

   Average Score: Total score divided by number of runs.

Glossary

SERIES: Several runs or experimental sessions that are grouped in accordance with the stated purpose and design of an overall experiment.

SESSION: A unit comprising all the trials of one test occasion.

SIGNIFICANCE: A numerical result is significant when it equals or surpasses a criterion of degree of chance probability. The criterion commonly used in parapsychology today is odds of at least 100 to 1.

SPONTANEOUS PSI EXPERIENCE: A natural, unplanned occurrence of an event or experience that seems to involve parapsychical ability.

STIMULUS: See TARGET.

SUBJECT: The person who is tested in an experiment.

TARGET: In ESP, the object or mental event to which the subject is attempting to respond; in PK tests, the objective process or object which the subject tries to influence (such as the face or location of a die).

    Target Card: The card which the percipient is attempting to identify or otherwise indicate a knowledge of.

    Target Face: The face on the falling die which the subject tries to turn up by PK.

TELEPATHY: ESP of the mental state or activity of another person.

TRIAL: In ESP tests, a single attempt to identify a stimulus object; in PK tests, a single unit of effect to be measured in the evaluation of results.

AN ESP RECORD SHEET

No. _____

Subject _____ Experiment _____

Observer _____ Date _____

Type of Test _____ Time _____

General conditions _____

Use other side for remarks.   Total score _____   Avge. score _____

With ESP cards use ∧ for star, o for circle, L for square, + for cross, = for waves.

1		2		3		4		5		6		7		8		9		10	
Call	Card	Call	Card	Call	Card	Call	Card	Call	Card	Call	Card	Call	Card	Call	Card	Call	Card	Call	Card

◎ SIGNET (0451)

KNOW THE PAST, THE PRESENT AND THE FUTURE!

- [ ] **WRITE YOUR OWN HOROSCOPE by Joseph F. Goodavage.** A leading astrologer tells how you can chart your individual horoscope with the accuracy of a trained professional. This ancient science is explained with explicit details and rare clarity that will unlock the secrets of your character—and your future—as no other book can. (130936—$3.50)

- [ ] **YOU CAN ANALYZE HANDWRITING by Robert Holder.** Here is the fascinating book that explains, stroke by stroke, the significance of every type of handwriting including that of famous public figures like Richard Nixon, Helen Gurley Brown and Walter Cronkite. A practical tool for self-knowledge and personal power. (137213—$4.50)

- [ ] **FORTUNE IN YOUR HAND by Elizabeth Daniels Squire.** Let this world-famous authority guide you into the realm of fascinating perceptions about the past and future, about yourself and others through the science of palmistry. (142322—$2.95)

- [ ] **1001 WAYS TO REVEAL YOUR PERSONALITY by Elyane J. Kahn, Ph.D. and David Rudnitsky.** This authoritative book by a prominent psychologist lets you use all your actions, preferences, and habits to tell you more than a mirror can about yourself and those around you. (140281—$3.95)

- [ ] **YOUR MYSTERIOUS POWERS OF ESP by Harold Sherman.** Explore the whole new world of your mind—and unlock the secrets of your own amazing psychic sensitivity! One of the world's great sensitives, writers, and lecturers on psychic phenomena explains why and how mind-to-mind communication is possible, exploring: telepathy, extrasensory healing, communicating with the dead, and out-of-body travel. With documented testimonies and case histories. (093151—$1.95)

Prices slightly higher in Canada

Buy them at your local bookstore or use this convenient coupon for ordering.
NEW AMERICAN LIBRARY,
P.O. Box 999, Bergenfield, New Jersey 07621

Please send me the books I have checked above. I am enclosing $_____
(please add $1.00 to this order to cover postage and handling). Send check or money order—no cash or C.O.D.'s. Prices and numbers subject to change without notice.

Name_____
Address_____
City_____State_____Zip Code_____
Allow 4-6 weeks for delivery.
This offer is subject to withdrawal without notice.